Poems Written
in a Time of Plague

Poems Written in a Time of Plague

Further Reflections on Scripture

TIM VIVIAN
Preface by Jack Hernandez

RESOURCE *Publications* · Eugene, Oregon

POEMS WRITTEN IN A TIME OF PLAGUE
Further Reflections on Scripture

Copyright © 2020 Tim Vivian. All rights reserved. Except for brief quotations in critical publications or reviews, no part of this book may be reproduced in any manner without prior written permission from the publisher. Write: Permissions, Wipf and Stock Publishers, 199 W. 8th Ave., Suite 3, Eugene, OR 97401.

The Preface is adapted from "Reflections on the Plague" by Jack Hernandez, The Bakersfield Californian, Community Voices, May 6, 2020 (online).

Scripture quotations are from New Revised Standard Version Bible, copyright © 1989 National Council of the Churches of Christ in the United States of America. Used by permission. All rights reserved worldwide.

Scripture quotations marked (NIV) are taken from the Holy Bible, New International Version®, NIV®. Copyright © 1973, 1978, 1984, 2011 by Biblica, Inc.® Used by permission of Zondervan. All rights reserved worldwide. www.zondervan.com. The "NIV" and "New International Version" are trademarks registered in the United States Patent and Trademark Office by Biblica, Inc.®

Resource Publications
An Imprint of Wipf and Stock Publishers
199 W. 8th Ave., Suite 3
Eugene, OR 97401

www.wipfandstock.com

PAPERBACK ISBN: 978-1-7252-8320-6
HARDCOVER ISBN: 978-1-7252-8321-3
EBOOK ISBN: 978-1-7252-8322-0

Manufactured in the U.S.A.   08/11/20

To all those who, with empathy and compassion,
against, it seems, increasing ever-accelerating odds,
work for truth, justice, and peace.
"Blessed are the peacemakers,
for they will be called children of God."

To
John Lewis
February 21, 1940–July 17, 2020

"He believed that in all of us, there exists the capacity for great courage, that in all of us there is a longing to do what's right, that in all of us there is a willingness to love all people, and to extend to them their God-given rights to dignity and respect."
—President Barack Obama

"Then the clouds gathered, the hour of storm, the power of darkness came, the sun got bloody red, Christ was crucified; and his enemies that loved darkness better than light triumphed that he was gone. On Easter Day this same sun had another rising."

—GERARD MANLEY HOPKINS, *The Sermons and Devotional Writings of Gerard Manley Hopkins*, 40

Suppose God shewed us in a vision the whole world enclosed first in a drop of water, allowing everything to be seen in its native colours; then the same in a drop of Christ's blood, by which everything whatever was turned to scarlet, keeping nevertheless, mounted in the scarlet, its own colour too."

—GERARD MANLEY HOPKINS, *The Sermons and Devotional Writings of Gerard Manley Hopkins*, 194

Contents

Preface by Jack Hernandez   xi
Author's Note   xv
Abbreviations   xxiii

I. TRIDUUM: HOLY FRIDAY, HOLY SATURDAY, EASTER SUNDAY

Lacrimae Rerum Lacrimae Gaudii	3
Triptych: A Sequence for the Triduum	4
Once Asleep, I Now Awaken	9
No Corpses Only the Risen	11
Overturning Adam's Curse	12
Now Crucifixion	13
Each Day to Calvary	14
Salve from His Open Wounds	16
Now Ash	19
Pietà	20
Forgiveness	21
I Saw Salvation Once	22
Witnesses	24
The Decision Each Makes	26
Wings Become Light	28

Her Afterbirth Itself Effulgence	29
From the Infant's Face	31
Jerusalem's Streets	32
Embers Into Flame	33
Fruit and Its Seed	34
Easter Ascensions Mary Magdalene	35
He Removes the Dirt from Her Skin	37
The Winged Shadows of the Dove	39
Questions of the Resurrection	40

II. LACRIMAE RERUM

Syllabaries Known Only in Silence	45
Our Sacred Cornerstones	46
One Transfiguration Will Never Be Enough	47
Each Ditch Sluiced with Pain	48
Across the Street	50
The Untoward of Indifference	52
The Further You Dig Into Origins	54
Holocaust, Holocaust, Fiery Consumer of Bones	56
One Angel Stricken	58
Barbed-Wire Ours	60
A Prophet of Dung	62
Joshua's Sun at Gibeon	63
Each Lazarus	65
His Tribe is Wilderness	66
This Scroll with Lacerations	68
Dare We This Day	70
And Still the Ancients Weep	73
Each Stone a Weight	75
Cradle Naming Stones	76
What Redemption	78

If Animals Could Be Criminal	80
Antipodal Savageries	81
From Sunup to Sun's Rest	82
The Judas Within	83
Soft Hearts Are Their Own Whips	84
Something Akin to Vision	86
May Tongues of Fire	88

III. LACRIMAE GAUDII

Christchild	93
That First Milk	94
Silence Bears God's Own Belief	96
Each Embrace Naked or Clothed	98
Against the Mean	100
The Lizard and its Bones	101
The Gate Within Christ's Agora	103
The Cure of Souls	105
Dance That You May Become	107
Each Tree Each Vine	108
Each Bone Will Find Its Lost Body	109
The Acts of Paul	111
This New Sabbath	116
Only Absolved Dare We Confess	118
His Wilderness Within	119
Birthed From God's Womb	121
Each Body Whole	123
A Single Piece of Skin	125
As the Holy Dove Now Descends	127
Deep Glowering Clouds Now Leaving	128
The Lord's Always Empty Throne	130
Scripture Index	133

Preface

LIKE SO MANY OF US, Tim Vivian was stunned by what happened in the winter and spring of 2020. First came the literal plague, COVID-19; and as we all socially distanced and sheltered from this devastating, deathly disease, another plague came, that of racial injustice and death. From this we have learned that plagues are both literal and metaphorical, as I have written in a piece published in our local newspaper.

The plague is real. The death, suffering, pain, and loss it brings are real. The loss of a parent or grandparent is real. The loss of a mother or father is real. The loss of a child is real. The loss of a friend is real. Many have lost jobs, income, and a sense of future. Many, isolated at home, have lost the close, warm connection with family, with friends, and with the world outside their front door.

Plagues bring death to humans, as they have to the millions who died in the Black Death of the Middle Ages and the Flu Pandemic of 1918. And as we face and reflect on the terrible reality of this current plague, we can in our time of waiting think about the plague in a different way, as well, think of the plague as a metaphor.

During this difficult, hermetic time, I have reread Albert Camus's *The Plague*. A novel, written in 1947, it describes what happens when a deadly plague strikes the French-Algerian town of Oran and how various people react to it, especially when the whole town is quarantined, is shut off from the rest of the country. Many think Camus saw the plague in this novel as a metaphor for fascism, how it infects people with its deadly ideas.

As I, like many of you, have adjusted to this hermit way of living, I have also thought about the plague as a metaphor, a metaphor for human existence: how humans cause the death of things like tolerance, love, truth, wisdom, nature's beauty, and authentic pleasure. And, of course, how we cause death through the plague of war.

Wars, and rumors of wars. I can't think of a time without wars. Especially now when we are so connected globally and daily hear about wars in other lands. Of course the last century saw millions die through World Wars I and II. And we almost obliterated ourselves in nuclear war . . . still a possibility. And not only do we die, but we have killed off many other living species through our reckless exploitation of lands and oceans. Even the planet is in danger through climate change.

And while we are free, many live under totalitarian regimes that forbid the freedom of thought and religion. When will that plague end?

Intolerance and hatred drive wars and their devastation. Political divisions and religious differences are but a few of the plagues of hatred that still rage in our midst. Oh, those others, they are so evil. Although we have eliminated the plague of slavery, we still spread the plagues of racism, sexism, homophobia, and more.

This current plague has once again exposed the plague of inequality. I grew up in Detroit where now many of those who have died are black and/or poor. We have not eliminated economic insecurity for many of those who work hard at minimum wage jobs, and who have no health insurance. We have not provided the homeless with shelter, food, and care.

We cherish our freedom, yet we live our ordinary, normal lives in the plague of consumerism, where we are infected with the need and desire to buy, buy, buy whatever is new, whatever promises us a fleeting, superficial glory and joy of the beads of success. We shine outwardly, and diminish inwardly.

What, then, can this plague teach us as we reflect in our stay-at-home time? Certainly, we must be even more conscious of our love of family and friends, our love of their voices and hugs. We must care for those who suffer from want and indifference. We must see the plagues we bring upon ourselves and others. To do this we must be aware of the carriers of our human plagues. In Camus's *The Plague*, the carriers are first rats, then people. For us the rats are too often those who use social media to spread hatred and untruth. We must, through reflection and spiritual growth, become immune to the hatred they spread.

Yes, we must grow our compassion for all of us, in our community, our nation, and our world. We must stop our plagues. As the poet W. H. Auden says in his poem "September 1, 1939," "We must love one another or die."

As Tim knows so well, and as his poetry in this book shows so well, the metaphors of poetry take us from the literal observations of the mind into the depths of our hearts and souls. This is done so beautifully in these stanzas from "Triptych: A Sequence for the Triduum," Part II, a midrash on Galatians 3:6–9:

So we often disagree? That's what we who
follow Torah do! Look at the Sadducees
and their hopeless denial. But many who
follow Jesus make everyone who differs,

or even dares a question, apostate, traitor.
Why? Abraham, Moses, Isaac, and Jacob
are our mutual fathers; Miriam and Sarah,
Zipporah, Rebekah, and Rachel our common

mothers. But . . . what from this grace do I
see? I see them dancing! All are dancing!
And Jesus! And Mary Magdalene! And with
each woman who midwifed Jesus transient!

Even Paul! He who bears still the weight of
so many chains, Paul now ventures onto the
dance floor. All of us are dancing! Our wine
is from Cana. We sing even shout Shema!

In unison and harmony! And, when the dance,
as it must, draws to a close, our hearts will
open wide. Now dead to our fears, we clasp
hands. Pilate, Judas, Caiaphas, come! Join us!

Such a powerful metaphor for unity, for us all to tear down the walls that separate us in this time of sorrow and healing, of conflict and love. To tear down the walls separating wealth and poverty, racism and equality, blind belief and seeking wisdom, stereotypes and truly seeing others. To joyfully be with all in the dance of life.

Such is the power of poetry. Such is the power of Tim Vivian's poetry.

JACK HERNANDEZ
Bakersfield, California

Author's Note

I WROTE MOST OF the poems in this volume between January and Pentecost Sunday, May 31, 2020, some before January, a few after Pentecost. Lent began in 2020 with Ash Wednesday, February 26, when COVID-19 had already invaded our borders and bodies, and now the nation's consciousness. As of February 26, two people in the U.S. had died of COVID-19. As I completed the manuscript of this book on the morning of June 15, 115,644 Americans had died from the plague. Responsible estimates are that in August or September, the death toll will be 200,000.

As if one plague weren't enough, on May 25, six days before Pentecost, police in Minneapolis murdered George Floyd, an unarmed black man, stopped for a $20 misdemeanor. Because of the previous murders of black men, and women, by whites,[1] especially police, this second plague hypostasized 400 years of the American plague(s) of slavery, Jim Crow, segregation, and racism.[2] Plague is both metaphor and physical presence. In May, the Rev. Dr. Otis Moss, III described the three men who killed Ahmaud Arbery while he was jogging in his Atlanta neighborhood in February as having tested positive for "Confederate COVID 1619—a disease," he said, "that is often asymptomatic; and spreads through human contact, rhetoric, ignorance, and family relations."[3] Never before had I thought of plague as sin. Or of sin as plague.

    1. See NPR, "A Decade of Watching Black People Die," May 31, 2020 (online); and Nicholas Quah and Laura E. Davis, "Here's A Timeline Of Unarmed Black People Killed By Police Over Past Year," May 1, 2015, Buzzfeed (online).

    2. See David W. Blight, "One Week to Save Democracy: Lessons from Frederick Douglass on the Tortured Relationship between Protest and Change," *The Atlantic*, n.d. (online). I certainly do not mean that the peaceful protests after George's death are a plague; the endemic and systemic wrongs in American society and structures, and the actions therefrom, are the plague.

    3. Moss, "The Cross and the Lynching Tree: A Requiem for Ahmaud Arbery" (online), cited by the Rt. Rev. Mariann Budde, "The Crucible of Justice," May 7, 2020

Thus the title of this volume, *Poems Written in a Time of Plague*, reflects two plagues. My hope as I finish this manuscript in mid-June is that the first plague has taught us about the good fruits of compassion and community and that the continuing non-violent protests following George's death will help birth a resurrection in the hearts, minds, and souls of all Americans, a new Easter.

As the 20th-century theologian Karl Barth astutely says, "The pastor and his congregation should not imagine that they are a religious society that is fixated [only] on certain themes, but that they live in this world. We do indeed need, according to my old formulation, the Bible *and* the newspaper."[4] In this volume, I have reflected in poetry on events from January to early June, 2020. The notes indicate many of my "newspaper" sources, most online. As with my first volume of poems, *Other Voices, Other Rooms* (Wipf & Stock, 2020), many of the poems here deal with difficult, here even awful, subjects but, as we see all too clearly these days, indifference, indecision, and denial and, infinitely worse, evil acts, have wreaked havoc on souls and bodies in America. As Vice President Joe Biden said at a memorial service for George Floyd in Houston:

> We cannot leave this moment thinking we can once again turn away from racism that stings at our very soul, from systemic abuse that still plagues American life . . . As [Supreme Court Justice] Thurgood Marshall once implored, America must dissent from indifference, it must dissent from fear, the hatred and mistrust. We must dissent because America can do better, because America has no choice but to do better.[5]

The subtitle of this volume, *Further Reflections on Scriptures*, indicates that the book is a follow-up to *Other Voices*.[6] I note in the Author's Note there that "All history is story." As Deborah Miranda says, "Story is the most powerful force in the world."[7] I read scripture as story—sacred story. The emphasis in the previous sentence is crucial. As Karen Armstrong points out,

---

(online). Eliott C. McLaughlin, "Ahmaud Arbery Was Hit with a Truck Before He Died, and His Killer Allegedly Used a Racial Slur, Investigator Testifies" (CNN, online). *The Cross and the Lynching Tree* is a harrowing, but necessary, book by James Cone; he shows that Christian lynchers and American Christians in general did not, or refused to, see the connection between lynching and the cross.

4. Barth, in an interview in 1966 (online), translation by Kim Vivian.

5. Bart Jansen, "'You're so brave.' Biden Speaks to Pain Felt by George Floyd's Daughter in Funeral Message," *USA Today*, June 9, 2020 (online).

6. Wipf & Stock, 2020.

7. Miranda, *Bad Indians: A Tribal Memoir*, xvi, emphasis hers; Vivian, *Other Voices, Other Rooms*, xvii.

"The gospels are not historical documents: they do not attempt to give us the facts of Jesus' life. They too are *midrash*, weaving scriptural verses together to create a story that injected meaning and hope into the perplexing present."[8]

Meaning and hope in the perplexing present. "Midrash" (plural *midrashim*), a Hebrew word, means "interpretation, study" of scripture. Further, it signifies exegesis and re-interpretation. All reading, and translating, is interpretation. Poets midrash scripture; a good one is Scott Cairns.[9] One of my favorite midrashim is a traditional song dating to the early 1900s, "Oh Mary Don't You Weep"; it interweaves the Exodus with Mary the mother of Jesus:

> Oh Mary, don't you weep, don't you mourn
> Oh Mary, don't you weep, don't you mourn
> Pharaoh's army got drownded
> Oh Mary don't you weep . . .
>
> Mary wore three links of chain
> Every link was Jesus' name
> Pharaoh's army got drownded
> Oh Mary don't you weep

In stanza eight, after much tribulation, the Exodus and Mary offer this hope: "Mary wore three links of chain / Every link was freedom's name."[10] Perhaps the greatest modern American midrash in verse is another song: "Go Down Moses," a song of liberation, ancient and modern:

> When Israel was in Egypt's land
> Let my people go
> Oppress'd so hard they could not stand
> Let my people go
>
> Go down, Moses
> Way down in Egypt's land
> Tell old Pharaoh
> Let my people go[11]

"Midrash" technically applies to rabbinic exegesis of scripture, especially in the Talmud. More broadly, all reading is midrashic. As a friend

---

8. Karen Armstrong, *The Lost Art of Scripture: Rescuing the Sacred Texts*, 218.

9. See Cairns, *Slow Pilgrim: The Collected Poems*.

10. "Oh Mary, Don't You Weep," traditional (online). I first heard Bruce Springsteen's rendition on *Springsteen, Live in Dublin: The Seeger Sessions*. A studio video is on YouTube.

11. For an introduction with bibliography and links, see "Go Down Moses," Wikipedia.

recently wrote to me, "I am re-reading some of the books that we studied in your [Religious Studies] classes. I find it so interesting how different a book can be the second time through. No, didn't mean that. It is I who am different, of course, so I view it through new eyes." My friend has captured an important truth. Frederick Streng further makes an essential point: "Religion is a *means of ultimate transformation* . . . An ultimate transformation is a fundamental change from being caught up in the troubles of common existence (sin, ignorance) to living in such a way that one can cope at the deepest level with these troubles. That capacity for living allows one to experience the most authentic or deepest reality—the ultimate."[12]

Transformation, daily metanoia, is essential to the religious life. For me, Greek *metánoia* (pronounced *meh-TA-nee-ah*) does not so much emphasize repentance (though, necessary, it does mean this) as it speaks of a change (*metá*, "beyond") of mind (*noûs* > -*noia*), a different way of looking at things, a new way of seeing—and being.[13] In 1953 the Jesuit and peace activist Daniel Berrigan stayed and studied at the Jesuit house of Paray-le-Monial in France; he writes movingly about his experience there, his *metánoia*:

> I felt in many cases . . . I . . . was being asked to operate in an entirely new way, to rebuild my senses, my very soul. It was not merely a matter of fumbling about with a new language and slowly gaining confidence in it. The truth was that the language offered new ways into the world of other human beings—and that these others, penetrated and formed by a thousand-year history expressed in their lucid and vivid language, were also new beings, into whose community I was invited to enter. The invitation was austere but irresistible.[14]

Aren't we all, if we're awake outside and within, daily learning a new language? And, as Berrigan with insight says, "fumbling about with a new language and slowly gaining confidence in it."

This volume has three sections: "I. Triduum," poems reflecting on the biblical events of Holy Friday,[15] Holy Saturday, and Easter Sunday vis-à-vis

12. Streng, *Understanding Religious Life*, 3rd ed., 2 (emphasis his).

13. I think I long believed this, but reading and teaching Greg Boyle's books crystallized it for me: Gregory Boyle, *Tattoos on the Heart: The Power of Boundless Compassion* and *Barking to the Choir: The Power of Radical Kinship*.

14. Berrigan, *Disarmed and Dangerous: Poetry, Drama, Prose*, ed. Michael True; cited in Jim Forest, *At Play in the Lions' Den: A Biography and Memoir of Daniel Berrigan*, 32.

15. Instead of "Good Friday," I am borrowing Spanish "Viernes Santo," "Holy Friday."

our holy and, especially now, our unholy plague-ridden days; "II. Lacrimae Rerum," poems about realities that cause tears (*lacrimae* < *lacrima*) deep in our heart and soul about things as they are (*rerum*); "III. Lacrimae Gaudii," poems that, amidst the carnage in our lives, celebrate goodness with tears of gladness and joy (*gaudii* < *gaudium*).

In addition to notes about "newspaper" sources, this volume supplies footnotes to most of the poems with brief glosses that explain and/or inform the reader about certain terms or provide sources for scriptural quotations and allusions.

    A suggestion: before reading a poem, the reader may first want to read the biblical passage that the poem is midrashing and, second, read the notes so she or he has extra food for the journey, having them in tandem with the poem.[16] I ask (well, tell) my students that when they're reading they should have their phones handy so they can use the web to look up people, places, and words. The notes here do some of that seeking and finding. My mantra for my students when they're studying—well, anything—is "Context, context, context." The notes with the poems provide at least partial context. Perhaps the greatest abuse of scripture now is reading—and, especially, proof texting—it without its context, which means, really, without its consent, or content.

    This volume also supplies a Scripture Index at the end for those who want to look up a passage in Scripture and find the poem or poems that employ it.

    I have done my best to use inclusive language. We students and readers always need to remember that what we call "inclusive language" was not a concern of the ancients (or, for some of us, even of our parents and grandparents). When I imagine these folks thinking or speaking, they often use language we would not. I have used masculine pronouns for "God" as little as possible. But we need to remember that that is the way the ancients referred to God.

    I have used throughout "Hebrew Bible" for the Jewish Scriptures rather than "Old Testament."

    The terms "BCE" (Before Common Era) and "CE" (Common Era) are more-inclusive scholarly terms for "BC" and "AD," respectively.

    All references to and citations from the Bible, unless otherwise noted, refer to the New Revised Standard Version (NRSV).

---

  16. A number of readers of *Other Voices, Other Rooms* have told me that the notes have helped.

I have followed the practice of the NRSV in using LORD when Jews, which also means the earliest followers of Jesus, speak of or to God. LORD, "Adonai," stands in for YHWH, the Sacred Name that Jews, out of respect, did not and do not pronounce (Exodus 3:13–15). The Septuagint (the third-c. BCE Greek translation of the Hebrew Bible, which all the New Testament authors use) uses Greek *kýrios* for Adonai. "Lord" is now the way we spell *kýrios*, which the first Christians used for Jesus. For ancient Christian readers of and listeners to the Septuagint, then, the *kýrios* they heard and enunciated sounded and symbolled both "LORD," God, and "the Lord," Jesus/Christ, thus providing a linguistic theology and Christology.

The symbol "//" indicates parallel passages within the Gospels, especially between Matthew, Mark, and Luke, the "Synoptic" Gospels.

An Abbreviations page, (p. xxiii), gives information on the abbreviations in this volume.

Writers read. While writing these poems then working on the manuscript of the book, I was reading the following books that spoke to me deeply. My thanks to the authors and editors for their words that have often comforted, challenged, and confronted me, thus inspiring—inspiriting—me.

- Karen Armstrong, *The Lost Art of Scripture: Rescuing the Sacred Texts*
- Margaret Atwood: *The Testaments*
- Andrew Bacevich, *The Age of Illusions: How America Squandered its Cold War Victory*
- Daniel Berrigan, *And the Risen Bread: Selected Poems 1957–1997*
- Gregory Boyle, *Barking to the Choir: The Power of Radical Kinship*
- Lawrence Cunningham, ed., *Thomas Merton: Spiritual Master*
- Jim Forest, *At Play in the Lions' Den: A Biography and Memoir of Daniel Berrigan*
- Scott Cairns: *Slow Pilgrim: The Collected Poems*
- Israel Finkelstein and Noel Asher Silberman, *The Bible Unearthed: Archaeology's New Vision of Ancient Israel and the Origin of Its Sacred Texts*
- Gray Henry and Jonathan Montaldo, eds., *We Are Already One: Thomas Merton's Message of Hope*
- Gerard Manley Hopkins, *The Poems of Gerard Manley Hopkins*, ed. Robert Bridges

- Peter Milward, S.J., ed., *Readings of the Wreck: Essays in Commemoration of the Centenary of G. M. Hopkins'* The Wreck of the Deutschland
- Thich Nhat Hanh: *Living Buddha, Living Christ*
- Kathleen Norris, *The Cloister Walk*
- Mary Oliver, *Devotions: The Selected Poems of Mary Oliver*

Writers do not write alone. As always, deep thanks to numerous people: for this volume, first to Jack Hernandez, friend and poet, for his Preface; to those who wrote me about poems in *Other Voices, Other Rooms*; to The Rev. Dr. Gary Commins and Gwen Hardage-Vergeer for reading the penultimate draft of the manuscript and offering corrections and suggestions; to Greg Boyle, Rick Kennedy, and Jeff Russell for writing comments for the back cover; and, for their financial support, Dr. Robert Frakes, Dean of the School of Arts & Humanities, and Prof. Steven Gamboa, Chair of the Department of Philosophy & Religious Studies, both at California State University Bakersfield. And, as before, many thanks to the wonderful people at Wipf & Stock who helped these poems into print.

TIM VIVIAN
Trinity Sunday, 2020[17]
tvivian@csub.edu

---

17. See the sermon for Trinity Sunday by The Right Reverend Mariann Budde (Washington National Cathedral. June 7, 2020, online).

Abbreviations

Bauer	Walter Bauer, *A Greek-English Lexicon of the New Testament and Other Early Christian Literature*, ed. Frederick William Danker, W. F. Arndt, and F. W. Gingrich, 2nd ed. (Chicago: University of Chicago Press, 1979).
BCE	Before Common Era = B.C. ("Before Christ")
CE	Common Era = A.D (Anno Domini, "In the Year of the Lord")
HB	Hebrew Bible/Christian Old Testament (NRSV unless otherwise indicated)
KJV	King James Version of the Bible
Lampe	G. W. H. Lampe, *A Patristic Greek Lexicon* (Oxford: Clarendon, 1961). archive.org/details/LampePatristicLexicon/mode/2University Press
Montanari	Franco Montanari, ed., *The Brill Dictionary of Ancient* Greek, English edition (Leiden/Boston: Brill, 2015)
NIV	New International Version of the Bible
NRSV	New Revised Standard Version of the Bible
NT	New Testament (NRSV unless otherwise indicated)

I. TRIDUUM: HOLY FRIDAY, HOLY SATURDAY, EASTER SUNDAY

Let him easter in us.
　　—GERARD MANLEY HOPKINS

LACRIMAE RERUM LACRIMAE GAUDII:[1] THE THIRD SUNDAY IN LENT, 2020

A Midrash on Matthew 27:50,
Luke 23:46, and John 19:30

To my Christianity class,
Spring 2020. Deep thanks.[2]

You'll find no tears here, other than
ours. Our Lord's we once collected in
pots and jars. Why is no one willing
to tell this to his survivors? Day by

day, sometimes each hour, we poured
them, filled, into the cistern, derelict,
behind Peter's home. Each occasion
of pouring, because his tears indwelt

the clay we dropped each vessel into
God's welcoming arms. Not one of
them broke. Like ships on newborn
seas, they floated, intact, even as

the next pot or jar fell heavenfrom
upon them. We marveled each time.
They call out to us: *The moment he*
rises, we will, each a resurrection.

---

1. The Latin phrase *lacrimae rerum* means "(the) tears of things," from Virgil's Aeneid I.462 (c. 29–19 BCE). Some recent quotations have included *rerum lacrimae sunt* or *sunt lacrimae rerum*, meaning "there are tears of (or for) things." *Lacrimae gaudii* means "(the) tears of (or for) joy/happiness/delight."

2. Kyle, Lauren, Leonardo, Cristee, Meridian, Elyaval, Taylor, Nirmal, Stephany, and Ruben.

TRIPTYCH: A SEQUENCE FOR THE TRIDUUM[3]
APRIL 9–11, 2020

To the Rev. Dr. Vern Hill, Who Brought the Triduum to Us,
Grace-St. Paul's, 2007–2015

I. The Place of God's Skull:
Simon of Cyrene Shortly After the Crucifixion

A Midrash on Matthew 27:32,
Mark 15:21, and Luke 23:26

Holy Friday[4]
April 9, 2020

Are the sleeves of this priest's vestments
seamed with not smoke but sweat, tears,
blood? A honeyed remembrance shows
me that all three have borne witness: once,

prisoner'd, I bore his cross to the Place of
God's Skull.[5] After the three have died and
been removed, I return, alone, to this place.
Called to care for fissures, disembowelments

of earth that the women's tears have creviced
here.[6] Yes, here it is: I knew in my heart, my
soul, in my valleys of dry bones,[7] that his
blood, too, would become that honey that I

---

3. Triduum: from Latin, "three days," Good/Holy Friday, Easter Eve, and Easter Sunday.
4. Instead of "Good Friday," I am borrowing Spanish "Viernes Santo," "Holy Friday."
5. The Place of / God's Skull: Matt 27:33//Mark 15:22//John 19:17 translate Greek *Golgothâ(s)* as "the place of the skull," reflecting the Aramaic and Hebrew for "skull."
6. The women's tears: for the Gospel accounts of the women at the crucifixion, see Matt 27:55–56; Mark 15:40; Luke 23:49; John 19:25.
7. My valleys of dry bones: see Ezek 37:1–14.

knew—or thought I knew—when I was young
and dreamed of becoming one of them, a priest
dressed in linen and the finest wine. But now
the honey that I gather here stings, it scorches,

and yet—How can this be?—it consecrates me.
Honey cannot speak—yet here commands me
to lie down, to spread its caustic sweetness all
over me. I am bound, Lord! Lord, deliver me,

now, at this hour of my death,[8] or I die eternally![9]
The ants of your earth, the stinging flies of your
air, will soon discover me.[10] They will devour me.
When the last one stings, may I, dead, awaken.

II. One Simple Transparent Moment

A Midrash on Matthew 26:48-49,
Mark 14:44-45, and Luke 22:47-48

Holy Saturday
April 10, 2020

One simple transparent moment will do,
Judas, just one. I'm gently tracing here
the internecine paths within this cobweb
that join the two of us. How does that

---

8. Deliver me, / now, at this hour of my death: see John 12:27.

9. Or I die eternally: see Rom 2:7; 6:23; among many.

10. The image of honey and stinging insects comes from the Greek version of the *Life of Paul of Thebes* by Jerome (c. 347–c. 420) where a Christian martyr suffers this torture.

children's rhyme go? The one about the
spider and the fly? Which one is you?
Which is me? Each is, you know, a thing
of beauty within God's vision. Always,

but most assuredly, shortly after sunrise
when each warp and woof is a tear in our
LORD's eye,[11] here the sunlight infilaments
each line and each open space as the fly,

dead, drained hollow and dry, now awaits
our resurrection. You and I, my dear friend.
As I was dying, I asked my Father to spare
you the horrible deaths that my followers

now prophesy.[12] *But the choice, as always,
is not mine*, he says. Then it is choice, mine,
and yours. I will soon ascend to my Father,
you will descend a pauper's grave. But when

the gravediggers arrive, my spirit will block
them with an immovable stone and its angel.[13]
Yours will be a demon claiming your bones.
But our angel, having cleansed them, will,

against our disciples' wishes, fly them home.

---

11. "Tear" here is not a tear that one cries but rather a rip, something torn.
12. The horrible deaths: Matt 27:3–6; Acts 1:16–20.
13. An immovable stone and its angel: Matt 28:2//Mark 26:3–5//Luke 24:2–4.

III. When the Dance Draws to a Close:
An Unnamed Pharisee Rises from the Grave

A Midrash on Galatians 3:6–9

Easter Sunday
April 11, 2020

I was a Pharisee. Although dead, I am
still.[14] Followers of Jesus pillory and
post us, and that is who we always will
be to those who follow him: stumbling

blocks.[15] Some taunts were his, but now
we're props that challenge *him*: to them
we're merely weak substitutes for Pilate,
Judas, and Caiaphas, all enemies within.

So we often disagree? That's what we who
follow Torah do! Look at the Sadducees
and their hopeless denial.[16] But many who
follow Jesus make everyone who differs,

or even dares a question, apostate, traitor.[17]
Why? Abraham, Moses, Isaac, and Jacob
are our mutual fathers; Miriam and Sarah,
Zipporah, Rebekah, and Rachel our common

---

14. I was a Pharisee ... I am / still: see Phil 3:5.

15. Stumbling / blocks: Matt 18:6–7//Mark 9:42//Luke 17:1–2. On the divorce between Jews and early Christians, see James D. G. Dunn, *The Parting of the Ways: Jews and Christians* (1999), and *The Parting of the Ways: Between Christians and Jews and Their Significance for the Character of Christianity* (2006).

16. The Pharisees affirmed an afterlife; the Sadducees did not.

17. Many Christians, so very human, very early saw, and defined, themselves against an "other," as all too many do now. See the Gospel of John's use of "the Jews" and the Pastoral Epistles (1 and 2 Timothy and Titus). For the nadir of heresiology, see *Panarion* (*Adversus Haereses; Against Heresies*) by Epiphanius (c. 310–320–403). See also *Katà Ioudaiôn* (*Against the Jews/Against the Judeans*), by John Chrysostom (c. 347–407).

mothers. But . . . what from this grace do I
see? I see them dancing! All are dancing!
And Jesus! And Mary Magdalene! And with
each woman who midwifed Jesus transient!

Even Paul! He who bears still the weight of
so many chains,[18] Paul, now ventures onto the
dance floor. All of us are dancing! Our wine
is from Cana.[19] We sing even shout Shema![20]

In unison and harmony! And, when the dance,
as it must, draws to a close, our hearts will
open wide. Now dead to our fears, we clasp
hands. Pilate, Judas, Caiaphas, come! Join us!

---

18. He who bears still the weight of / so many chains: see Acts 16:26; 21:33; 26:29.
19. Our wine / is from Cana: see John 2:1–11.
20. Shema: Deut 6:4, "Hear, O Israel, the Lord our God, the Lord is one."

ONCE ASLEEP, I NOW AWAKEN: THREE DAYS BEFORE JESUS' ARREST

A Midrash on Matthew 4:25, 5:1, and 7:28, among many

In a dream, recent, someone shouted out
pathogen, and then someone yelled out,
even louder, perhaps even in desperation,
antipathogen.[21] My Greek, although not

educated, is usually good enough now
for the street and the marketplace: I had
some idea of the first word; of the second,
less. In this telling and silence I am now

in an open area, a great expanse (there are,
here, to my surprise, and its astonishment,
not only no Roman soldiers, but no foreign
invaders at all. In Jerusalem, in our time,

how is this possible?) There is a crowd. One,
standing by me, when I ask her (yes), tells
me that the whole population has come out,
here, to hear a prophet—and, she adds, much

more than a prophet.[22] But how can this be?[23]
In a dream, one anterior, another woman
informed me that, because of our apostasy,
insatiable, no more prophets would come.

---

21. Pathogen: "any disease-producing agent, especially a virus, bacterium, or other microorganism." Greek: literally "producing suffering."
22. A prophet—and . . . much / more than a prophet: Matt 11:7–9; Luke 1:76.
23. But how can this be?: see Matt 19:26//Mark 10:27//Luke 18:27.

I remember now—I wept. But why, then, am
I not rejoicing, dancing, now? I want to, and
badly. I look at him, with hope. Before I turn
back to ask the woman, I first say to myself,

within my dream, that this woman, in here,
is—no, not part of me, but me, deep within.
And, I see now, near without. When this our
prophet, although speaking, hears *without*

(Did I, just now, speak aloud?), he stops. He
turns to me. *Yes*, he says, *both*. Then, as I try
to wake up, he leans over me and touches me,
gently, on the shoulder. I awaken, bleeding.

NO CORPSES ONLY THE RISEN: THURSDAY IN EASTER WEEK 2020

A Midrash on Psalm 8, the Psalm for This Day's Readings

What young, impossible, easements
have newly begun their entrance here
into shadow, then darkness, and their
often-unrequited hope and struggle for

light? *Unrequited*—a masculine noun
with a feminine birth name: the first
breath she draws, her mouth and nose
cleared of the womb's desire to keep

her children to herself.[24] But the Lord's
womb, ever full, ever emptying, must
first embrace its boundaries, exigent
circumstance, before daring to go out

to bear others, fraught deliverance.
She is both future and remembrance.
When they know one another and, in
joyous coupling, give us to ourselves,

let us, please, summon our knowing
and unknowing. Dark spiders dance
on webs between them. But all our
mornings no corpses, only the risen.

---

24. Greek and Latin, like Spanish, French, and German, are gendered languages. Some nouns with masculine endings are feminine, such as Greek *ē odós*, "path" or "way," and some nouns with feminine endings are masculine, as Spanish *el día*, "day."

OVERTURNING ADAM'S CURSE: A DISCIPLE AFTER JESUS' ARREST AND EXECUTION

A Midrash on Genesis 3:17–19 and Romans 5:12–14

What, or whose, sudden interest has brought
Death near me now—too near—after I thought
I too had escaped by running away with all my
brothers?[25] Are they, craven, hiding together,

just waiting for someone—even a passerby
with the news of Jesus' capture, his chained
and pocketed betrayal—someone who schemes
with gold aurei to betray them?[26] The women,

terrified yet faithful, were heading to his tomb;
fearful, I betrayed myself with lepers' clothing
and followed them, safe, with Sinai's distance.[27]
Such remoteness soon constricted choked me;

it began to suffocate me the closer I drew to
his tomb. I had to sit down to breathe. I may
have become unaware. I awoke because of the
noise, clamor and cry they made, sandaled feet

slapping Roman pavement, gasps, cries and, yes,
shouts of amazement and gratitude and wonder,
not even holding their dresses out of the dust.
They knew they were overturning Adam's curse.[28]

25. Running away with all my / brothers: Matt 26:56//Mark 14:50.

26. Jesus' capture, his chained / and pocketed betrayal: Matt 26:47–56//Mark 14:43–50. Aurei, sing. *aureus*: a gold coin of Rome issued from the first-century BCE to the beginning of the fourth-century CE.

27. Betrayed: see Matt 26:47–56//Mark 14:43–50//Luke 22:47–62//John 18:1–11, 15–18.

28. Adam's curse: other than in Genesis, Adam and Eve together do not appear in the HB and only rarely in the deuterocanonical books (Tobit, Sirach, 2 Esdras), and

NOW CRUCIFIXION

A Midrash on Mark 14:50 and Matthew 26:56

One after another, they've fled. We
don't need to: we have wombs. Here
together we can find ourselves. In
that difference lies definition and thus

our differentiation and its stillborn
twin who pleads and sorrows for our
breasts, whether full or empty. I can
say all this now only because they've

fled. Flight, you see, can be assurance.
Observe the flight of carrion birds over
the fields, or in our homes, or in our
hearts: these now consecrate our blood,

always emulate of our swords, or spears,
or arrows. Then these weapons set about
building altars to our battlefields: each
body once resurrection now crucifixion.[29]

Adam appears in the Gospels only in Luke's genealogy (3:38). The disciple is expressing an early Christian understanding (Rom 5:12–14; 1 Cor 15:22; 1 Tim 2:13–14).

29. Altars to our battlefields: see Josh 8:1–31a. Daniel Berrigan: "Love your enemies? The Word of God in our midst? But we are at war! ... The time is short. Reject the errant history, the pseudo-tradition. There can be no just war. There never was one" (from *Testimony*; cited in Jim Forest, *At Play in the Lions' Den: A Biography and Memoir of Daniel Berrigan*, 274). See recently Tim Vivian, "The Bomb(s) This Time: A Meditation on Thomas Merton's *Cold War Letters*," and Gary Commins, "Cold War Letters to Our Cruel World," *Cistercian Studies Quarterly* 55.1 (2020): 19–54 and 55–76, respectively.

EACH DAY TO CALVARY

A Midrash on John 19:34

To Pamela Cranston

You don't send tears any more.
That's not a complaint, nor is it
fear's closest friend, sniveling.
When you were among us and,

at times, within, I would dry
them on my apron, my skirt,
the blanket I carried from your
birth. The clothes I would wash,

the blanket never. It is now so
full of holes that light lives within.
Every day I hung out so much of
my soul on this line—so much

that neighbors began to ask each
other, not me, how I was doing.
I'm doing well. Fine, thank you.
But only you and I understood

that my tears—and, yes, most
often, yours—were (impossible,
I know) not merely enslaved
carpenters crafting cross-staves,

but each woman at a well now
filling the evening's bucket with
its blood and water.[30] Each one,
in her knowing, as she walks

home, walks indirect, even far
out of her way, to sprinkle this
mixture on the streets and paths
that walk us each day to Calvary.

---

30. Each woman at a well: see John 4:1–7.

SALVE FROM HIS OPEN WOUNDS: THE LAMENTATIONS OF JEREMIAH[31]

*A Midrash on Matthew 27:56,
Mark 15:40, and John 19:25*

Everything we write
turns into elegy, and every elegy
slips into our own.

—Scott Cairns, "Another Elegy"[32]

He's as dead as I am now. Only
he knows the difference. I'm as
alive as he will be when he comes
and salves wounds in each of us.

Although for some reason the
writers ignore me, I, Jeremiah,
was with him at the foot of the
cross.[33] Each woman did her best

to shelter me, though I still wear
bruises and three bones broken
that don't, and may never, heal.
Elegy, a Greek word, explains

---

31. Lamentations "consists of a series of five poems on the destruction of Jerusalem in 586 BCE," written after the destruction and exile. "Although one very ancient tradition ascribes Lamentations to Jeremiah, practically unanimous modern critical opinion holds the book to be anonymous." See Delbert R. Hillers, "Lamentations, Book Of," *The Anchor Bible Dictionary*, ed. David Noel Freedman, 4.137a–41b; 137a–38b.

32. Cairns, *Slow Pilgrim: The Collected Poems*, 6.

33. I, Jeremiah, was with him at the foot of the / cross: see Matt 28:1//Mark 16:1//Luke 24:10//John 20:1.

lament, which calls us to bemoan,
bewail, and even regret. I once
saw some words that the Prophet
Jeremiah was speaking. The rabbi

who held the Prophet's script
allowed me to see only the very
top of the scroll. From what I can
remember (soldiers also kicked

me in the head), only individual
words, they were these (his words
spoke our beautiful poetry): *lonely,
widow, vassal, weeps bitterly,* and

enemies.[34] We are our fiercest
enemies. And we are also long
surrounded by adversaries, living
and dead, and those to come, the

booted footfalls and the clatter
of chariots, weapons, and horses.
We here, unlike our dear mother
Jerusalem, have no tears, bitter

or sweet.[35] As you see, he's as
dead as I am now. But I'm as
alive as he will be after he rises.
This is what our prophets tell

---

34. See Lam 1:12.
35. See Lam 1:2.

us, though not those standing
in the marketplace or before the
city's gates. I see here only now
that the lepers, lame, and blind,

the beggars and the unclean, and
even the prostitutes, are, like me,
first dead, then alive. Each has
wounds and cuts that bleed and

ooze. At dusk each day, as Rome's
soldiers change the guard, Jesus
rises; each woman at his side, he
works salve from his open wounds.[36]

---

36. Each woman at his side: see n. 6. Open wounds: see Luke 24:39–40.

NOW ASH: A DISCIPLE TO HIMSELF IMMEDIATELY AFTER THE CRUCIFIXION

A Midrash on Matthew 26:56

"Then all the disciples deserted him and fled."

Each reflection that I see in this mirror
that God holds up to me, whichever way
I turn, or don't, or walk backwards into
myself, is both accusation and its truth.

Why has God handed me this window
that never looks outward into light and
light's forgiveness, but only inward,
where failed sacrifice lingers, now ash?

PIETÀ: AT THE FOOT OF THE CROSS

*A Midrash for One of Jesus'
Followers after the Crucifixion*

Who will be the mother for each
of my sorrows? Each breath I take?
Who is she who will gather my lips
to her breasts? I cannot, even if I

could, and wanted to, gather them
to me here.[37] My wrists and my feet
bleed.[38] I know that I will never get
the taste of sour, bitter, wine out of

my mouth.[39] This wine still tastes of
the manure that Roman soldiers
shove my face into. But it could've
been worse. And why are all our

donkeys braying? Why am I now at
home gathering the few, pitiful, herbs
and spices I have here?[40] If I had any
children at home, I'd take the bread

out of their mouths so I could feed
him. But . . . I haven't had wine here
in weeks.[41] Where will I find one
mother for even one of my sorrows?

---

37. Here: see Matt 27:55–56//Mark 15:40//Luke 23:49//John 19:25.

38. My wrists and my feet / bleed: In the *Life of St. Francis of Assisi*, Saint Bonaventure reports that in 1224 Francis, after receiving a vision, received the stigmata, the wounds of Jesus, in his hands and feet.

39. Sour, bitter, wine: see Matt 27:48//Mark 15:36//Luke 23:36//John 19:29.

40. Herbs / and spices: see Mark 16:1//Luke 23:56; 24:1//John 9:40.

41. Bread...wine: Matt 26:17–30//Mark 14:12–26//Luke 22:7–39//John 13:1–17:26.

FORGIVENESS: AFTER THE CRUCIFIXION, A DISCIPLE, A SCRIBE, REFLECTS

A Midrash on Mark 16:8

This disunity that light brings home
startles me. The stars overhead both
glisten and terrify. I am not myself
here—but then, since his execution,

I am not myself anywhere. In God's
future—not my present—they will
call those like me *alienated*, from
Latin *alienus: unfriendly, inimical,*

hostile, suspicious. Some of these
I do not understand, yet they define
me, within. My interior fiends have
abandoned me. Once outside, they

now sport atop a cross. This I cannot
comprehend.[42] But I know I will that
new day when spikes incarnadine and
enfleshed come to kneel before me,

asking, impossibly, my forgiveness.

---

42. Comprehend: see John 1:5, "The light shines in the darkness, and the darkness did not overcome it." "Overcome" is *katélaben*, from *katalambánō*: (1) "win, attain" (1 Cor 9:24, Rom 9:30); (2) "gain control of, catch up with, seize" (Mark 9:18); (3) "surprise, catch, detect" (John 8:3); (4) "understand, grasp" (Acts 25:25) (Bauer 519b-20a). For John 1:5, Bauer 520b(4b) recommends (1) and (2), but I think all apply. It's a profound statement to say that the darkness has not yet understood/grasped the light. Perhaps someday it will; perhaps someday ours will, too.

I SAW SALVATION ONCE:
DISCIPLES GATHER AFTER THE CRUCIFIXION

*A Midrash on Matthew 12:9–14,
Mark 3:1–6, and Luke 14:1–6*

*For Elaine, who feeds the hungry and clothes
the naked on the streets of Bakersfield*[43]

I see now that this day has furthered
its despair. We sit beside a fire without
flame outside the city whose darkness is
now ours. No one dares to speak, no one

will get up to bring back the flame. *All
of us have deserted him,* one of us says.
Except me. We know that he, like us,
is a liar. The look on his face reassures

us. His face ours. *What will we do now?*
one asks, his head down, scratching for
flame. *If one of us here would get up,*
another says, *maybe we could be saved.*

I saw salvation once, another now says.
*A donkey, defeated, heavy-laden, lay
astride the side of the road. Its owner,
forsaking his possessions, had run off.*

*I expected people then to crowd the body,
plunder it, even pillage its rib cage. But
no one moved. Then, of a sudden, they
resumed their journeys. Save one. She*

---

43. Feeds the hungry and clothes the naked: see Matt 25:31–40, esp. vss. 34–36.

bends down. She places a cloth soaked in water across its brow. She then offers another cloth, of wine and water, to the animal. It sucks. She lies down beside

the beast, caressing its ears until it dies.

WITNESSES: MARY MAGDALENE, AFTER THE CRUCIFIXION, SPEAKS WITH MARY, THE MOTHER OF JESUS

A Midrash on 1 Corinthians 15:26

"The last enemy to be destroyed is death."

Now is a good time: I want to know
Death: I'll bear his son, stillborn.[44] We
now possess both his promise and its
forfeiture. *Who are we but witnesses*

of another giving birth within our soul,
our souls bearing the children of others—
we, long past menopause, long past, it
seems, the LORD's desire to beget his own.

If I could couple with myself, I would.
But what would such union, and disunion,
bring? I cannot say. My child, whether
female or, female's birthing, male—both

are memory: her beauties and longings,
her giving, often weeping our horrors.[45]
Horror I see every day beside morning's
bread, sorrow the food that consumes me

---

44. I want to know / Death: in biblical Hebrew, "to know" can also be a euphemism for knowing another sexually.

45. Memory: in the Greek of the NT, "memory," *mnḗmē* (English "mnemonics"), is a feminine noun.

each evening. At night the creatures whom we will never understand, even if we name them,[46] descend: they crawl, fly, and sting without our permission, grace, or betrayal.

This day is now crawling to its unimagined end. We sit here, you and I, with language, and yet our lips scarcely give meaning. But I see the words gather on your lips, orphan

children seeking their homes. *Yes, Mary, we will feed them, bathe them, and make clothes for them out of the nothing we possess—and yes, sister, they, made holy, will be our own.*

---

46. Even if we name / them: see Gen 2:20.

THE DECISION EACH MAKES: AFTER THE HARROWING OF HELL[47]

A Midrash on 1 Peter 4:6
and Ephesians 4:9

Gaufrido clarissimo magistro amicoque

The most unsettling thing about
the resurrection is that afterwards
God has fallen asleep, exhausted
by all his manifold labors to bring

Jesus up from the harrows of hell,
the cries, shrieks, and screaming
of all those who grasp and claw
at his feet as he begins his ascent.

The blood-given shrieking and
the unceasing wailing cause his
ears to bleed, the clawing tears
layer after layer of skin from his

feet, then his calves and thighs.
His blood now serves as rain for
all the plants beneath the earth
desiccated by the pain of denial

and blame. Perhaps all this can
explain why there are no angels
of silver wings, no gold-winged
archangels, no seraphim, not one

---

47. On Jesus' harrowing of hell, the Wikipedia entry offers a good introduction.

cherubim to welcome him. Only
one distraught, newly-appointed
servant of God standing watch
for hours until relieved, bone in

one hand, love, compassion, and
forgiveness in the other. Each
time the cellar door slams open,
he shows one palm, then the other.

WINGS BECOME LIGHT

A Midrash on John 20:17

The blackbirds sing cacophony in the desert
palms now forgiven. What do their dialogues,
their disagreements, say? Are they prophets?
Our priests? Or are they the slaves that each

morning unsewer our streets, sweeping our
offal into unseen alleyways and ditches?
The resurrection, I know, is near. But first
came slaughter and occupation. They deny

they are death, each power and dominion,[48]
but each one knows he is charnel. These
blackbirds now silence and fly away. They
leave no entrails to haruspex, no bones to

clatter and divulge God's natal misgivings.
Each blackbird, once present, now flown,
bears across its wings the crucified Christ.
As Christ ascends, the wings become light.

---

48. Power and dominion: Col 1:16; Eph 6:12.

HER AFTERBIRTH ITSELF EFFULGENCE: A DISCIPLE ON THE SABBATH MORNING BEFORE THE RESURRECTION

A Midrash on John 1:1–9

With thanksgiving for Rowan Williams, 104th Archbishop of Canterbury

I once needed, with almost every
breath I took—I once needed to
candlelight each known measure
of this darkness that is always

among and within. I'm not talking
about the light that resurrection
will bring, the bright new moons
around everything animate and

not, everything that calls itself
dead or living. I'm not talking
about that light. I'm speaking
here—to myself, to you—about

that light that dwells always, from
before we were born,[49] far within,
between not only the boundaries
between skin and bone but, from

the womb, the light that hibernates
between the intersections of our
being, in captivity, waiting, long
awaiting, both first birth and last.

---

49. Before we were born: see Jer 1:5.

Within this my supplication she's
making her way without pain from
far between bone and its protection
into Mary's birth canal.⁵⁰ At first

fearful of another darkness, she now
prays. Her benediction now tells her
that, since she herself is the very light
that Christ visioned when dying, she

must descend the birth canal. Because
she is light, she both envisions, and
is, light, both its appearance and, far
within, her afterbirth, itself effulgence.

---

50. She's / making her way: in Greek, "light," *phôs*, is a neuter noun; in Latin, however, *lux* is feminine, as in Spanish *la luz*. I am also imagining light here as the Shekhinah (a feminine noun in Hebrew), God's "Presence." See n. 176.

FROM THE INFANT'S FACE: SHORTLY AFTER THE RESURRECTION

A Midrash on Gehenna[51]

Feral dogs compete for scraps of food
outside Jerusalem's gates in the garbage
dump known as Gehenna, our one and
final magistrate. Despite his resurrection,

I still must wonder—what I see each day
requires it: Does each of us live there,
fighting the dogs and jackals for meat?
Sometimes they fight over what's left

of a baby, exposed.[52] We know only now:
Christ gives birth, here, each infant's face.

---

51. Gehenna: see Matt 5:22, 29–30; 7:13; 10:28; 13:38–42; among many. The NRSV and NIV, following the KJV, misleadingly translate "Gehenna" as "hell." For an introduction, see "Gehenna" on Wikipedia.

52. Babies, especially females, were sometimes "exposed," left either to die or be claimed by someone, often as slaves; see Lucius' Romans, "Why Were Newborn Children Left to Die in Ancient Rome" (online, with bibliography). See also T. M. Lemos, "Did the Ancient Israelites Think Children Were People?," Biblical Archaeology Society (online).

JERUSALEM'S STREETS:
TWO DISCIPLES AT THE CRUCIFIXION OF JESUS

A Midrash on Matthew 27:55–56,
Mark 15:40, Luke 23:49, and John 19:25

The pale declivities of fear are
ransom. For what, I'm never sure.
Lest we now make too much of
our fears, let us pause and count

each spike in his crown of thorns,
the weight of each Roman nail that
separated flesh from friend and, in
craft, avoided any path of blood

that would make this death sudden
and, thus, not satisfactory. *But each*
memory we held has now departed
from us. We looked at one another

in absence. What we had now was
present, and presence was too much
for us to bear. So those of us below
his cross, after the Romans had left,

tore off our clothes, down to our
naked souls. Breasts and lower
regions now exposed, we began
to dance. No, our dancing wasn't

open to all, designed to capture
the flesh of others, it was maternal,
a childbirth, our breast milk now
flowing through Jerusalem's streets.

EMBERS INTO FLAME: EASTER 2020

A Midrash on Matthew 28:1–10

What stone vocabularies newly
quarried sit upon each tongue
as we sing Alleluias to our risen
Lord who will still each day die

for us?[53] We beget our own time
of plague that forgives no one
but itself. And yet this day one
angel fans embers into flame.

---

53. Each day die / for us: see 1 Cor 15:3, "For I handed on to you as of first importance what I in turn had received: that Christ died for our sins in accordance with the scriptures." My midrash on this is that Christ died, and dies, *because of* our sins.

FRUIT AND ITS SEED

A Midrash on Luke 24:1–12

Ask your thoughts to be silent. Then
awaken. What did you learn, friend,
Spirit-inflamed?[54] *The space between
his crucifixion and our resurrection*

*is where we will learn the most. Yes,
yes, you're right—we have his deeds
and words. But did you know: with
each thing he did he birthed a dying?*

*Many of these died stillborn, but most
broke open and bore both fruit and its
seed. Then, with him no longer here,
together, sitting before an empty tomb,*

*we witness each die and rise again,
resurrection, now returned, our own.*

---

54. Spirit-inflamed: see Acts 2:1–4.

EASTER ASCENSIONS MARY MAGDALENE: TEN YEARS AFTER THE CRUCIFIXION AND RESURRECTION

A Midrash on Luke 8:2–3; Mark 15:40; 16:9; Matt 27:55–56; John 19:25

Please tell me, Lord, the importance
and instruction of this anniversary, the
day of your death and new birth born,
now each new day, each hour, and yet

dying the same. Claudius (yes), who
knows how to fathom the stars, tells us
that at both sunset and its rise the sun
is yours, and yet ever ours.[55] Possession,

as you often said, is hindrance.[56] But,
what is the difference here? When I
awoke this new morning I had been
carrying oils and spices to your still-

angeled tomb.[57] But this morning, I
now see, this crypt is no longer ours.
I heard that one winter's day a priestly
family found it empty, brought the bones

---

55. Emperor Claudius ruled the Roman Empire from 41–54 CE.

56. Possession, / as you often say, is hindrance: see Matt 6:19–21; Matt 19:24//Mark 10:25//Luke 18:25.

57. I was as usual / carrying oils and spices to your still- / angeled tomb: see Matt 28:1–10; Luke 23:54–56; 24:1–10; John 20:1.

of all its ancestors dating back to Aaron.⁵⁸
But Moses, our brother and yours, was
not among these. As I left the tomb in
this dream, this vision, I saw our Aaron

ascend, a golden calf bearing him to you.⁵⁹

---

58. A priestly family . . . / its ancestors dating back to Aaron: see Exod 28:1–4, 41, among many.

59. A golden calf: see Exod 32.

HE REMOVES THE DIRT FROM HER SKIN: THE WOMEN RUSHING BACK FROM THE TOMB[60]

A Midrash on Luke 8:40–56

What denizen now glistens outside in his
armor in the marketplace is a decision
that Rome makes. The Romans make all
the decisions, even when we live and die.

Their statuary is everywhere, some of them
clothed, some of them naked. This morning
I saw some of us shackled and chained to
pedestals, just below genitals and breasts.

Or was I dreaming? Or . . . maybe a vision,
sent to me by my angel? I try to remember.
But I did go outside, didn't I? Didn't all the
women, rushing back from the tomb, seize

me and push me up against the wall?[61] One,
when I resisted, even grabbed me by the
balls. When I shrieked, Salome[62] released
her hand. She began to weep. Now another

comes to us, in tears. She tells us that the
tomb is now empty. *Jesus,* she says, *is now
risen! Risen! The stone has rolled away! He
sits beside it.* "Lord," I ask, "What is this?"

---

60. The Women Rushing Back from the Tomb: Matt 28:1–10; Mark 16:1–8; Luke 24:1–12.

61. Seize / me and push me up against the wall: see Mark 14:50; John 20:19.

62. Salome: Mark 15:40; 16:1.

His hands and his feet are torn and bloodied. In his hands he holds a dove.[63] *He now blesses and frees it. And now, suddenly, there is a child! He is holding her in his lap; she is still*

wearing her burial shroud, now dirtied. With his tears he removes the dirt from her skin.

---

63. Dove: see Gen 8:8–12; Matt 3:16//Mark 1:10//Luke 3:21–22//John 1:32.

THE WINGED SHADOWS OF THE DOVE: A QUATRAIN FOR THE MONDAY AFTER THE THIRD SUNDAY OF EASTER IN A TIME OF PLAGUE

A Midrash on Psalm 74:19

"Do not deliver the soul of your dove to the wild animals;
do not forget the life of your poor forever."

After your death I set out alone.[64] The winged
shadows of the doves that we kill will remain:[65]
Is everything that we touch now felony? Yet
those you heal say you and I are now twinned.

---

64. After your death I set out alone: see Luke 24:13–14; the story of Jesus on the road to Emmaus (Luke 24:13–35) is the Gospel reading for this Sunday (Year A).
65. The winged / shadows of the doves: see Pss 55:6 and 68:13.

QUESTIONS OF THE RESURRECTION: ONE WEEK AFTER THE MURDER OF GEORGE FLOYD[66]

A Midrash on Matthew 6:28–29 and Luke 12:27

In Memoriam Philip and Daniel Berrigan, Prophets, Disciples, and Peacemakers 1923–2002, 1921–2016[67]

You don't get crucified for considering
the lilies of the field, their natural and,
unnatural, beauty. Now that we have his
resurrection, and our own, will those who

follow remember this? Our landscape,
both in terrain and interior, our Roman
roads lined with crosses, those beneath
rending their clothes, beating their breasts.

Will those who follow us remember this?
Will those who follow welcome the poor
as one of us, as one of them? Will they then
consider lepers as lilies, the hemorrhaging,

and the dispossessed? Will they touch them,
breastfeed them, as he did, placing his hands
within their wounds in order to feel his Father
within? Will they carry Lazarus, almost dead,[68]

---

66. See "What We Know About the Death of George Floyd in Minneapolis," *The New York Times*, May 27, 2020 (online).

67. For an excellent, powerful reflection on the brothers Berrigan, see Jim Forest, *At Play in the Lions' Den*.

68. Lazarus: Luke 16:19–31.

from his gate, the dogs still licking his sores,
and seat him first,[69] stinking of urine and shit,
at the banquet he would never be invited to?
Will they? Will they listen to these words?

Although I am long dead I stand beside
them, resurrected. Will they, unbelieving,
question me to make sure that I, as they, am
one of Adam's own, Eve's lifetime sorrow?

Will you accept that Eve died because of our
sins?[70] Will you turn away when she tells you
that the cities you live in you have built with
Cain?[71] Will you, disbelieving, gather stones

with which to stone not her, but yourselves?[72]
Will you, when Jesus reminds you of your
evil, one by one drop your weapons—only to
send your slaves each night to remand them?

---

69. The dogs still licking his sores, / and seat him first: see Luke 16:20–21 and Matt 22:1–14; Luke 14:7–12; Matt 19:30//Mark 10:31.

70. Will you accept that Eve died because of our / sins: see 1 Cor 15:3.

71. The cities you live in you have built with / Cain: see Gen 4:17.

72. Will you, disbelieving, gather stones: John 8:1–11.

II. LACRIMAE RERUM [73]

"It demands great spiritual resilience not to hate the hater whose foot is on your neck, and an even greater miracle of perception and charity not to teach your child to hate."

—JAMES BALDWIN, "LETTER FROM A REGION IN MY MIND," THE NEW YORKER, NOVEMBER 17, 1962

"Remember this, O Lord, how the enemy scoffs . . .
Do not deliver the soul of your dove to the wild animals;
do not forget the life of your poor forever.
Have regard for your covenant,
for the dark places of the land are full of the haunts of violence.
Do not let the downtrodden be put to shame;
let the poor and needy praise your name."

—PSALM 74:18–21

---

73. The Latin phrase *lacrimae rerum* means "(the) tears of things," from Virgil's *Aeneid* I.462 (c. 29–19 BCE). Some recent quotations have included *rerum lacrimae sunt* or *sunt lacrimae rerum*, meaning "there are tears of (or for) things."

SYLLABARIES KNOWN ONLY IN SILENCE: WRITTEN IN A TIME OF PLAGUE

A Midrash on Deuteronomy 28:20 and 28:28–29

We sang all afternoon and evening
to our shadows until we discovered
that their shadows, long our own,
are deaf. We then asked of Deafness,

as if, distant, in a medieval village,
to ring church bells once and ever.
Rung, all the villagers gather to us
to hear our Lord and Savior's near

supplications. One woman brings
her child in utero in order to instruct
her in God's syllabaries known only
in silence. A farmer comes in from

fields to cradle his deaf, dumb, and
blind child in hope of three miracles.
Shadows and their interpreters now
descend our steepled church walls,

a fearful child in flight down a ladder,
the hay loft now alone. The barn burns.
Lightning strike. All the animals flee to
rescue except one, refusing to be moved.

OUR SACRED CORNERSTONES

*A Midrash on Matthew 24:1–2,
Mark 13:1–2, and Luke 21:5–6*

What sacred cornerstone temples
here? What words do we have that
dare speak of a cornerstone's wound,
its self-betrayal, the dust and ashes

it finds on the street, feeding itself
each day as we begin the sacrifice?
Before we slay each victim, cut its
throat, we search the mouth for gold.[74]

Cornerstones, hungry, require fresh
meat. Flesh eaten always very rare
offers again silent, bleeding protest,
then closes its eyes, spirit ascended.

Those who eat sacrifice build empires.
They consecrate churches.[75] As these
empty each Sunday a lone sacristan,
unresurrected, leaves open the doors.

---

74. In the Nazi death camps, prisoners extracted the gold teeth from the dead. A haunting novel on one such camp, its inmates and supervisors, its living, dead, and walking dead, is Erich Maria Remarque, *Spark of Life* (1952).

75. See Michelle Boorstein and Sarah Pulliam Bailey, "Episcopal Bishop on President Trump: 'Everything He Has Said and Done is to Inflame Violence,'" *The Washington Post*, June 1, 2020 (online), and Tom Gjelten, "Peaceful Protesters Tear-Gassed To Clear Way For Trump Church Photo-Op," NPR, June 1, 2020 (online).

ONE TRANSFIGURATION WILL NEVER BE ENOUGH

*A Midrash on Matthew 17:1–20,
Mark 9:2–8, and Luke 9:28–36*

Tuesday, February 18, 2020
Day 1125 of the Trump Administration

One Candlestick of Compassion still burns—
no, it flickers, and her opposing gales grow
more obsessed each day with what they grab
and consume together: children within their

embrace grow hungrier each day and friends
lie within cages.[76] One transfiguration will never
be enough. Jesus is atop a high mountain, alone
except for two followers, their clothes dazzling

white. Their fear now ours, we lie awake both
day and day's night, with our children crying
not beside, but within us.[77] Even so, we plead
anacusis.[78] The wounds from our deafness and

lack of sight bleed. We rub and rub the creams
we merchandise for our health. Strong winds,
co-creators, sweep over the face of the waters.[79]
Seeking compassion and justice, they drown.

---

76. Friends / lie within cages: see Jennifer Rubin, "Actually, Trump and his Party Don't Care about the Kids in Cages," *The Washington Post*, July 29, 2019 (online).

77. Zach Tilly, "The Trump Budget is Bad for Children," Children's Defense Fund, n.d. (online).

78. Anacusis (Greek *a-*, a negative, + *akoúō*, "to hear") is complete deafness.

79. Winds, / co-creators, sweep over the face of the waters: see Gen 1:2, "In the beginning when God created the heavens and the earth, the earth was a formless void and darkness covered the face of the deep, while a wind from God [or: "while the spirit of God" or "while a mighty wind"] swept over the face of the waters."

EACH DITCH SLUICED WITH PAIN: THE SEMBLANCE OF A SELF

A Midrash on Matthew 16:25

To Thich Nhat Hanh,
Living Buddha, Living Christ[80]

"But if the truth is to make me
free, I must also let go my hold
upon myself and not retain the
semblance of a self which is an
object of a 'thing.'"[81]

The terrors that one flesh brings
can lie with another and make
yet more. Oneness can itself be
terror until each dies to its own.

There's no need now for shock or
anger: being silent is ever its own
salve. Don't ever offer to buy it.
Across the street, where mothers

await one—even one—sign of
liberation, it's free. Only—don't
ask for it. Do you see? These our
mothers have no children here

---

80. Nhat Hanh with others practices "Engaged Buddhism": "Engaged Buddhism, or 'socially engaged Buddhism,' denotes the rise of political activism and social service by Buddhist communities and organizations in Asia and the West since the 1950s" (AcademicRoom, "Engaged Buddhism," online); see Nhat Hanh, "The Fourteen Precepts of Engaged Buddhism" (Lion's Roar, online).

81. James Finley, *Merton's Palace of Nowhere*, 142; see 157, n. 32.

to breastfeed. No, they express
our need for the self to die into
pottery broken, then thrown onto
each soul's trash heap. Now, as

carrying water home from wells,
each shoulders her pot into each
prison we name our self, each
ditch sluiced with pain, our own.

ACROSS THE STREET

*A Midrash on Ephesians 6:5–6
and Colossians 3:22*

*To Eric Barle who, bless
him, asks such questions*

It's not so much that we do
wrong but that we do it so
often, and so well.[82] I sit
here against a Roman wall.

I hold out my hand in hope:
I'd welcome even a lepton[83]
with ΗΡΩΔΟΥ ΒΑΣΙΛΕΩΣ,[84]
though it would probably burn

my hand. But maybe I could
eat the scar, a tasty Herodian
delicacy! Thank you, Missus,
for these fine crusts of bread.

---

82. "Trump's $4.8 Trillion Budget Would Cut Safety Net Programs and Boost Defense," *New York Times*, February 10, 2020 (online): "President Trump released a $4.8 trillion budget proposal on Monday that includes a familiar list of deep cuts to student loan assistance, affordable housing efforts, food stamps, and Medicaid, reflecting Mr. Trump's election-year effort to continue shrinking the federal safety net."

83. Lepton: "The *prutah* (plural, *prutot* or *prutahs*) was the most common denomination of coins in ancient Israel from the Hellenistic period up to the destruction of the second Temple [in 70 CE]. The *lepton* (plural, *lepta* or *leptons*) is one half of a *prutah*. *Prutah* is a Hebrew word. *Lepton* is a Greek word . . . We now know that the smallest ancient Palestinian coin denomination was the *lepton* or half *prutah* . . . Thus, the *lepton* as the 'poor widow's mite' [Mark 12:41–44, KJV] seems to accurately reflect Mark's account." See David Hendon, *Guide to Biblical Coins*, fourth ed., 34–37.

84. ΗΡΩΔΟΥ ΒΑΣΙΛΕΩΣ: Hērṓdou Basiléōs, "of King Herod," "King Herod's": Herod the Great, 74/73 BCE–4 BCE, was client king of Judea from 37–4 BCE. The title appears on some of his coinage.

May the LORD bless us with
many more! It's been, what,
hours now? I cannot—no,
I will not—eat. Across the

street a doulodidáskalos⁸⁵ has
been beating his slaves male
and female until each bleeds.
He at last turns and looks at

me. *You! Beggar! Come here!*
Bring your bread. Dip it in these
wounds, their blood the finest
*garum; if you wish, liquamen.*⁸⁶

---

85. Doulodidáskalos: "slave master."
86. Garum, sometimes called *liquamen*, "was a basis for many Roman cooking sauces, condiments, and main dishes. Scholars use 'garum' to refer to fish sauces generally . . . *Garum* was made from salted [fish] blood and viscera." See Michael Decker, "Garum and Salsamenta," in *The Oxford Dictionary of Late Antiquity*, ed. Oliver Nicholson, 1.642a.

THE UNTOWARD OF INDIFFERENCE: SATURDAY, APRIL 3, 2020

A Midrash on Luke 16:19–31

In Memoriam those who died because of the president's inaction January–March, 2020

"The Trump administration received its first formal notification of the outbreak of the coronavirus in China on Jan. 3. Within days, U.S. spy agencies were signaling the seriousness of the threat to Trump by including a warning about the coronavirus—the first of many—in the President's Daily Brief. And yet, it took 70 days from that initial notification for Trump to treat the coronavirus . . . as a lethal force that had outflanked America's defenses and was poised to kill tens of thousands of citizens."[87]

The untoward of indifference is its
bone, its second nature, the home
from which colonies of demons each
hour descend and descend,[88] always to

return with more than they first bore,
with each dead body now less. *But
more is always less!*[89] Complacency's
denizens encamped at fee now dance

---

87. Yasmeen Abutaleb, Josh Dawsey, Ellen Nakashima, and Greg Miller, "The U.S. Was Beset by Denial and Dysfunction as the Coronavirus Raged," *The Washington Post*, April 4, 2020 (online). As of the writing of this poem, June 4, the United States, with 4% of the world's population, has 1/3 of the world's COVID-19 deaths. See Eugene Jarecki, "Trump's covid-19 inaction killed Americans," *The Washington Post*, May 6, 2020 (online).

88. Descend and descend: see "Jacob's Dream at Bethel," Gen 28:10–22; the line here is an inversion of v. 12.

89. But / more is always less!: See George Orwell's Ministry of Truth in his novel *1984* (1949). The Ministry uses a language, "Newspeak," that is really doublespeak: "War is Peace. Freedom is Slavery. Ignorance is Strength."

around the bone. A knock now on the
door. A bejeweled survivor of those
who descend, lazily indifferent, with
difficulty gets up. Inebriated not with

wine but with the pain he ignores
each hour, he steps over dead Lazarus
lying in fragments before the gate.[90]
He ambles slowly to the door, each

step pausing lazily to scratch his balls
and yawn. When he reaches the entry,
the entrance is not locked but aflame.
Now turning his back, he yawns again.

---

90. Thomas Mockaitis, "Working Poor Will Suffer the Worst Health and Economic Effects of COVID-19," March 18, 2020, *The Hill* (online).

THE FURTHER YOU DIG INTO ORIGINS: A MIDRASH ON A POEM BY DANIEL BERRIGAN[91]

May 12, 2020

After being tested and found safe,
we dug a grave on the White House
lawn, then another, and another.
Then they arrested us.[92] In fact, they

had handcuffed us much earlier but,
cuffed, we had continued digging
until we dug 83,366 holes, and then
more for ourselves.[93] Still manacled,

we lay in them. And the little shovel,
a small infantry spade, circa 1898
or '99 when we, all of us, invaded
Cuba and the Philippines, later got

museumed, but without photos of our
digging. And no memento of the later
extractions. With us held captive,
God's industrious angels went on

---

91. "Zen Shovel," in Berrigan, *The Risen Bread: Selected Poems, 1957–1997*, ed. John Dear, 232–33. See Lee Moran, "Washington Post Editorial Issues Dire Warning To Trump Aides 'Enabling His Incitement,'" *Huffington Post*, June 3, 2020.

92. Dan Berrigan, with others, was arrested, jailed, and imprisoned many times, including at the White House, for acts of civil disobedience or, as he might say, sacred obedience: pouring blood on draft files, burning draft files, and hammering on unarmed nuclear warheads, among many. See Jim Forest, *At Play in the Lions' Den*.

93. We dug 83,366 holes: the cumulative number of deaths in the United States from COVID-19 on May 12, 2020.

excavating. Down down he dug, down and down, up up she piled the blood-receptive spoils. Done, the angels now whisper to each of our puzzled souls:

> *The further you dig into origins, deeper and deeper the origins get.*[94]

---

94. Origins: see "The White House Was, in Fact, Built by Slaves" (*Smithsonian Magazine* online): "Slaves were likely involved in all aspects of construction, including carpentry, masonry, carting, rafting, plastering, glazing and painting . . . And slaves appear to have shouldered alone the grueling work of sawing logs and stones."

HOLOCAUST, HOLOCAUST, FIERY CONSUMER OF BONES

A Midrash on Joshua 6:
The Slaughter and Destruction of Jericho[95]

"480,000 people have been directly killed
by violence over the course of these conflicts
[in Iraq and Afghanistan], more than 244,000
of them civilians."[96]

What calefaction here reinvents
our bones? So many dead. Here.
To bury them in this desecrated,
disfigured earth would cause our

LORD's wrath to awaken (it does
so so easily) and slaughter us.
Immediately, and freely. So we,
by our Joshua's order, will build,

from the ruins of their once-city,
a holocaust[97] normally reserved
for oxen, sheep, and birds, their
hide, wool, feathers now our own.

---

95. Jericho: see Israel Finkelstein and Noel Asher Silberman, *The Bible Unearthed*, Chapter 3, "The Conquest of Canaan," 72–96.

96. Murtaza Hussain, "It's Time for America to Reckon with the Staggering Death Toll of the Post-9/11 Wars," *The Intercept*, November 19, 2018 (online), based on Brown University's Costs of War Project.

97. Holocaust: a religious animal sacrifice completely consumed by fire: Greek *holókaustos* from *hólos*, "whole," + *kaustós*, "burnt." Hebrew: *korban olah*; see Exod 20:21 and Lev 1:10–11, among many. See nn. 109 and 159.

These dead bodies that I bear, I
now see, are my newborn skin,
itself somehow aflame. But why
is there no self-conflagration, no

immolation? One of the dead,
only partially burned, arises. She
holds out her still-enfleshed hand
and caresses her pregnant belly:

*You, dear soldier (dead, I can say
this now), you and I are lovers,
belovèd. When you enter me, and
my dead flesh envelops you, we*

*two are each a sacrifice for your
holocaust: "Holocaust, holocaust,
fiery consumer of bones, whose
repulsive scent ascends towards*

*God's throne, lash each of our
enemies with your fiery tongue."*
Her words embrace me. With her
husband slaughtered, what can I

do? I swaddle our newborn child.[98]

---

98. Swaddle: see Luke 2:7 (KJV): "And [Mary] brought forth her firstborn son, and wrapped him in swaddling clothes, and laid him in a manger because there was no room for them in the inn."

ONE ANGEL STRICKEN

A Midrash on Luke 10:25–37

I. This I Would Find Acceptable

I have, at last, begun to look
for myself beneath this ditch.
Although the night is falling
deeply all around me, and the

jackals have begun braying for
their dinner, which includes me,
I will smile and announce that
our belovèd LORD, in his finite

wisdom, has prepared for me
here a comfortable bed, such as
David slept and adulterated in.[99]
This I would find acceptable.

II. A Stricken Tree

That was my first inclination,
my first denial—and its betrayal.
And the second was like unto it:
love my neighbor, this trough,

as myself. On this second Mosaic
commandment hang all of Torah
and all the LORD's prophets.[100]
Each depends a stricken tree.[101]

---

    99 A comfortable bed, such as / David slept and adulterated in: see 2 Sam 11:1–27.
    100. And the second was like unto it / . . . and all the LORD's prophets: Matt 22:39 (KJV then NRSV).
    101. Each depends a stricken tree: see Deut 21:23.

III. But Now I Am

My third, as people staying far
distant pass me by, some even
afraid to look at me, as though
sight itself could suffer dismay,

this third—now I *am* fearful—
is to realize that I, as I dig
deeper, recoil from myself.
I never weep, and won't now.

IV. Each an Angel Stricken

My final understanding, as God's
jackals, now silent, draw near,
is that when I die, here, alone,
the flesh they will fight over and

pull from my bones, the blood
they will drink from me as holy
altars purl our deliverance from
each victim's gore—when I die,

my wife, my children, even my
so-called friends, will sit at my
table, celebrate my life. When
we're well on our third, or into

our fourth, even fifth, cup, I too
will raise a toast: *Had I had all
of you with me in the ditch, we
would all be one angel, stricken.*

BARBED-WIRE OURS

*A Midrash on Matthew 9:36,
Mark 6:34, and Luke 24:44–49*

One consequence of terrible sin
is, no, not regret, nor regret's twin,
shame, but exultation, laudatory
embrasures that long fortify both

without and within the battlements
that extend across a barren landscape,
roads lined with crucifixion. Guards
stanchion each wound, every breath.

Breath here, and always, is Spirit.[102]
But she and her mother, Ruach, will
ever decline to attend these our slave-
owners' auctionings. It is we who

wear shackles, chains as best-dressed
mummery: each soul now prays while,
indifferent, it watches a caterpillar that
awaits carrion beak. Meat that demons

throw to us in handfuls. Lord, will you
embrace us always rancid, and forgive?
Some, awake, will ask *Can both be true?*
Truth now awakens, far away from our

---

102. Breath, here and always in the Bible, is also spirit: Hebrew *ruach* and Greek *pneuma* mean "wind," "breath," and "spirit." *Ruach* is a feminine noun. See nn. 169, 187, and 217.

line of sight. She knows our homicide.[103]
Since she does, she foresees each lying
word, each prevarication, first as prick,
then as gouge, then disembowelment.[104]

Mourning, she dresses now in clothing
only a slave would wear. As each sinner,
bejeweled, rejoicing, takes the throne,
she, to our astonishment, begins to sing.

She sings as she and forgiveness must.
Each sleeps
    always
        atop
            barbed-wire
                fences.

---

103. Truth . . . / She: Greek *alḗtheia* is a feminine noun, as is *áphesis*, "forgiveness," below. Etymologically "truth" means "not (*a-*) forgetting" (*lanthánomai*).

104. Disembowelment: Greek *splanchnízomai*, "to have compassion," is cognate with *tà splánchna*, "guts." In Hebrew, "compassion" is cognate with "womb." *Splanchnízomai* is the verb the NT uses when Jesus shows compassion.

A PROPHET OF DUNG: JEREMIAH, FROM THE CISTERN

A Midrash on Jeremiah 8:1–2, 9:22, 16:4, and 25:33

I confess: a prophet of dung am I.
No—my confession is what *they*
make excrement. I sit here anyway.
As adversaries prophet, king, and

peasant are one and the same: Baal
adulterers, roasting their children
on spits for Moloch.[105] He is fasting:
they bring wine and eat his flesh.

Huldah is both prophet and friend.[106]
She has long prophesied, as have I.
So why am I punished in this cistern?
No water, only mud.[107] So, then, this

dreck: their sins, or mine? Or both?
Huldah, can you hear me? Throw me
a rope. No? Then Huldah, come swim
with me until God saves, or we drown.

---

105. Baal / adulterers, roasting their children / on spits for Moloch: see Jer 2:23; 7:9; 19:15. Moloch: see Lev 18:21; 20:2–5.

106. Huldah: see 2 Kgs 22:14–20; 2 Chron 34:22–28.

107. So why am I punished in this cistern? / No water, only mud: see Jer 38:1–6.

JOSHUA'S SUN AT GIBEON

A Midrash on Joshua 10:1–15

Please listen to me: the sun is now
shadowing beyond its means, which
forewarns that those who live only
in nearest-darkness learn very early

to love only their darkness. Not
friends, not husbands or wives,
nor even their children, who, they
now realize to their indifference,

and perhaps ours, are an unwonted
gray, bones buried far too long in
fields drear with wheat and rye long
turned under. Joshua's sun at Gibeon,

coruscated with blood and slaughter,
has long worshiped a God I wish I
could forget, or at least hide from:
each luster of light, every glister,

has for illicit centuries given birth
to lamentation and wailing, dark
ululations from long-conquered and
shadowed bones, a toothpick used

once by Joshua's God and thrown
away. By night dim umbras draw near
and gather them, bushel baskets full
that they return to Ai and Jericho.[108]

The cities' late-dismembered stones
now wood build fires and burn them.[109]

---

108. Ai: see Josh 8; Jericho: see Josh 6.
109. Burn: burning is a key word in Israelite sacrifice: see Exod 20:24; 29:14; Lev 1:1–17; among many. See nn. 97 and 159 on "holocaust."

EACH LAZARUS

A Midrash on Luke 16:19–31

Sanctified sailors, drowned, now walk me
far across this landscape, detritus of dry
alluvials. They teach me about those things
I understood but, with them, now find that

I no longer do. And, even more, never did.
Understanding, I'm beginning to see, is
wretched Lazarus lying before each gate.[110]
I once went up to each one, handed each

a small coin, absolved myself, and escaped.
I understand now, only much later, that each
one held two things: first, each Lazarus had
inscribed in Aramaic his lesions upon each

wall. Second, each Lazarus had something
in his hand, his hand fisted. When, looking
away, I held out what I had, he pried open
the closed hand with the other. Now freed,

he handed me this coin, my visage effaced.[111]

---

    110. See Benjamin Oreskes, "Mass Unemployment over Coronavirus Could Lead to a 45% Jump in Homelessness, Study Finds," *Los Angeles Times*, May 14, 2020 (online).

    111. In the occupied Palestine of Jesus' day, Roman coins often carried the visage of the emperor; see n. 84.

HIS TRIBE IS WILDERNESS: AFTER THE DESTRUCTION OF SODOM AND GOMORRAH[112]

A Midrash on Exodus 17:1–7[113]

Nothing beside remains. Round the decay
Of that colossal Wreck, boundless and bare,
The lone and level sands stretch far away.

—Percy Bysshe Shelley, "Ozymandias"

We stones here remember and dismember
against ourselves. Many of us now lie dead
or silent or, in silence, fearing that when the
vultures come, not to strip us to our bones

(we have none), but to load us on carts ever
drawn by oxen and mules, carried proximate
and distant, we will have to atone for sin, not
ours but yours, by remembering palaces and

walls, dormitories built for fratricide armies[114]
and, here to keep things honest, brothels and
latrines. Some of us now line your cloacal
alleys each with its offal. Each of us, dead,

---

112. This poem has as its provenance one time when I was walking through a medieval town in Provence. At the corner of one street I happened to look down at the bottom of a building. I saw that its cornerstone had Latin on it—and was upside down. I got on my knees and read the inscription. I no longer remember what it said, but the moment, the image, the *Sic transit*, have stayed with me many years.

113. On Sodom and Gomorrah, see Gen 18:6–19:29.

114. Palaces and / walls, dormitories: see the discussion of the ninth–eighth-c. BCE Omrides in Samaria in Finkelstein and Silberman, *The Bible Unearthed*, "Palaces, Stables, and Store Cities," 180–86.

silent, or afraid, wants to know: Where will
I be next? Will I, possibly, go from sewer to
calligraphed monument, or to royal rooms
where I will hear far too little, and too much?

We lie here in desert sands and their sunstroke.
(Do we not bleed?)[115] Those sequestered too far
into fragment will remain. But—who knows?
Within millennia, perhaps, a desert tribe, sent

by a God, or gods, will wander here. All our
tribe, except those now disintegrate, dying of
oblivion, will cry out together to our saviors:
Why did you bring us here only to allow us to

die in anger, retribution, and their loneliness?
When he hears us, their leader will take up his
staff. He strikes one of us. Then he strikes one
more. Then another. And another. When our

water breaks at last, his tribe is wilderness.[116]

---

115. Do we not bleed?: see Shakespeare, *The Merchant of Venice* III.1.1287–1307, spoken by Shylock, "the Jew."

116. His tribe is wilderness: see Exod 14:11.

THIS SCROLL WITH LACERATIONS: A PHARISEE SOON RABBI JUST AFTER THE FALL OF JERUSALEM, 70 CE

A Midrash on The Jewish Wars *6.9*
Written in a Time of Plague

"But when [the Romans] went in numbers
into the lanes of the city with their swords
drawn, they slew those whom they overtook
outside, and set fire to the houses where the
Jews had fled, and burned every soul within
them, and laid waste a great many of the rest;
and when they came to the houses to plunder
them, they found in them entire families of
those dead, and the upper rooms full of corpses."[117]

I would like, dear LORD, to stretch
to horizons your impossibilities, not
as obiter dicta but as answers to our
questions answered yet here not heard.

For example: that rainbow you long
ago gave birth to that exsanguinated
the dying breath of each person, each
animal, drowning beneath your curse.[118]

And those impairments made of skins
you sewed for Adam and Eve.[119] Holy
Torah teaches us that our progenitors
knew each other only east of a flaming

---

117. Flavius Josephus, *The Wars of the* Jews (or *Jewish Wars*) 6.9 (Project Gutenberg online), slightly modernized.

118. That rainbow . . . / drowning beneath your curse: see Gen 9:8–17.

119. Skins / you sewed for Adam and Eve: see Gen 3:21.

sword protected by sacred cherubim.[120]
So, dear LORD, did you teach them also
how to remove the dead animals from
around their newfound loins, not only

to pass urine and feces but to grapple
with one another not in conflict but
with that pleasure you first felt when
they exulted, kissed, and caressed one

another in your holy and yet to forgive
name? Their each cry and whisper we
here understand, yet ever misprision.
My LORD, I sit with your holy Torah

that yesterday I fled with hefted across
bare shoulders. I sit here now in view
of these our executed ruins. Weeping,
and pleas, the execrations of these our

dead, reach me here. I put wool in my
ears, and yet I descry them. Tell me,
LORD, what holiness, what sanctuary,
can now comfort and sustain us?[121]

That silence we hear is the restraint
of crackling wood and bone. If I now
open this scroll with lacerations that
offer you forgiveness, what shall I do?

---

120. A flaming / sword protected by sacred cherubim: see Gen 3:24. In biblical Hebrew, "to know" can be a euphemism for having sexual relations with another.

121. What sanctuary, / can now comfort and sustain us: during the destruction of Jerusalem, the Roman soldiers destroyed all but one wall of the Temple, now called the "wailing wall."

DARE WE THIS DAY

*A Midrash on Matthew 27:32–56,
Mark 15:21–41, Luke 23:26–49,
and John 19:17–37*

"I need a song that forgives me.
I need a song that forgives my lack
of forgiveness."

    —Deborah A. Miranda[122]

He looks away. Disarray his.
Absent his Lord, he touches
his beard. Our Gospel writers
will not ask either him, or us,

why. Why always belongs
to imagination. Imagination,
long after, will not be able
to grasp, or even grapple

with, spikes pounded far into
flesh, a crown of new thorns
lacerating a dying forehead,
a spear thrust into the side

birthing water and blood for
the Eucharist.[123] So, then, we're
back to touch. Can *Why?* now
require less of us? A woman

---

    122. Miranda, *Bad Indians: A Tribal Memoir*, 176.
    123. Water and blood for / the Eucharist: John 19:32–34. At the Eucharist many priests add a bit of water to the chalice filled with wine. "Eucharist" (Holy Communion, the Lord's Supper) comes from Greek *eucharistía*, "thanksgiving."

touches the fringe of Jesus'
clothing.¹²⁴ He touches a leper,
who immediately is cleansed.¹²⁵
He touches Peter's mother-

in-law: her fever leaves her;
she gets up and begins to
serve and minister to him.¹²⁶
There are others, almost too

many to name. Most don't
tell us where a touch happens.
This is where our imagination
returns. An archeologist now

hands us a spike, unearthed
in far-off Palestine.¹²⁷ When
we, afraid, touch it, a woman's
hemorrhage discovers healing,

a leper now remembers what
it is to be clean. Though clean,
he now refuses to ascend the
Temple steps to offer sacrifice.¹²⁸

---

124. A woman / touches the fringe of Jesus' / clothing: Matt 9:20–26//Mark 5:21–43//Luke 8:40–56.

125. He touches a leper, / who immediately is cleansed: Matt 8:1–4//Luke 7:1–10//John 4:43–54.

126. He touches Peter's mother- / in-law: Matt 8:14–15//Mark 1:29–31//Luke 4:38–41. "Serve," *diakoneō* (English "deacon") also means "to minister to."

127. A spike, unearthed / in far-off Palestine: see "A Tomb in Jerusalem Reveals the History of Crucifixion and Roman Crucifixion Methods," Biblical Archaeology Society, July 22, 2011 (online).

128. A leper, being unclean, was not able to offer sacrifice at the Temple.

This is where he learns what refusal means. Thus he, our need, needs our healing. Dare we, this day, now touch him?

AND STILL THE ANCIENTS WEEP: WRITTEN IN A TIME OF PLAGUE

May 3, 2020

*A Midrash on Joel 1:1–12
and Deuteronomy 28:38–43*

The fruit is setting now in this valley
that for centuries we've called Queen
Sheba's Paradise: figs, grapes, olives,
and pomegranates.[129] So many armies

imperial and mercenary have marched
through here and again. The bones of
our ancestors stay silent throughout
the winter (their voices may be in the

wind), but come spring with its yearly
singing and dance they speak to us in
each seed that we plant, each harrow
held in fear and hope. These together

with barley and wheat are the bread we
eat, the watered wine we drink late each
day, our wine drunk full and sweet come
Sabbath when the LORD sits to eat with

us. And still the ancients weep, to warn
us of battle-geared armies. Will the LORD
our God come drown these?[130] Or will he
take the bread from our mouths, leaving

---

129. Queen Sheba: see 1 Kgs 10:1–13.
130. Will the LORD / our God come drown these: see Exod 14:26–31; 15:1.

us gore as our only remembrance? Will
our newborns at the breast find only this
blood? What color the tears they weep?
Too many questions. But our ancestors

ask, and so I speak. Prophet Elijah long
ago rode a chariot of whirlwind to heaven.[131]
When his chariot at last returns, will you?[132]
Will seeds we plant return bread, or dust?[133]

---

131. Prophet Elijah long / ago rode a chariot of whirlwind to heaven: see 2 Kgs 2:1–12.

132. When his chariot at last returns: see Mal 4:5–6. Many Jews expected the Messiah to return alongside Elijah. At the Passover celebration meal Jews leave an empty chair for Elijah.

133. Will seeds we plant return as bread, or dust?: see Deut 28:24.

EACH STONE A WEIGHT

A Midrash on John 8:1–11

Once you hammer judgement, and its
fears, into stone, you will hammer
another, and another, until you have
stones enough to stone an adulteress.[134]

She is, though, although you won't
admit it, at least not here, and, most
likely, never to yourself, ever, she is
the one lay you lust for the most: she

refuses your lecheries—no, not just
your own, but ours, each of us, blind,
a stone in each hand, each stone now
a weight that, held, defines our being.

---

134. Adulteress, *pórnē*: Greek *porneía* (English "pornography") has a broader meaning than the usual translation of "adultery," "prostitution" (Montanari 1724b): "prostitution, unchastity, fornication, immorality" (Bauer 854a-b), "illicit intercourse, lewdness" (Lampe 1121b).

CRADLE NAMING STONES: THREE DISCIPLES IN CONVERSATION

A Midrash on Luke 13:34 and Mark 13:1–2

May 28, 2020

"United States Coronavirus (COVID-19) Death Toll Surpasses 100,000"[135]

I. Cradle

I've helped cradle more than one
newborn, both mine and all those
misbegotten, conceived not in sin
but within sin's twin, indifference.[136]

II. Naming

But why indifference? Isn't it our
greed that soldiers an army set free
that slaughters everyone in sight,
then renames the dead the living?[137]

III. Stones

A freedman, my masters pay me,
although so very little, to gather
stones for each stoning. Defiant,
I gather pebbles. But when I come

---

135. CDC, May 28, 2020 (online).
136. Indifference: see "The Untoward of Indifference," p. 52.
137. Katherine Schaeffer, "Six Facts about Economic Inequality in the U.S.," Pew Research Center, February 7, 2020 (online).

back into town and lay them at
my masters' feet, they pour water
over each. Each time, we watch
pebbles grow into stones that kill.

WHAT REDEMPTION

A Midrash on Job 33:28

"GOD is in CONTROL"
—a neighbor's yard sign later removed

To Jack Hernandez

One consequence of emergency
is dereliction. Incompetence is
its twin.[138] Let's sit down. Is a cross
carried condemned an inmate of

crucifixion? Or is its impalement
resurrection? Convicted and yet
manumitted? But the plagues that
dwell among us and within will all

hold their tongue when questioned.
So, this leaves us where? Should
we visit prophets who prophesy
our sins as both victims and their

---

138. One consequence of emergency / is dereliction. Incompetence is / its twin: see "The Missing Six Weeks," *The Guardian*, March 28, 2020 (online): "The president was aware of the danger from the coronavirus [almost from the beginning]—but a lack of leadership has created an emergency of epic proportions." Paul Waldman, "Republicans Now Want Us To Embrace Mass Death," *The Washington Post*, May 7, 2020 (online): "It's almost impossible to overstate what an appalling dereliction of duty it is that the Trump administration, having screwed up its pandemic response so spectacularly, is now essentially washing its hands of the whole effort, no longer bothering to try to enact a coordinated nationwide testing and tracing system, and just telling everyone to get back to work."

adulatory midwives? Of course, but only when they listen to each of us here. *Will last now be first, although transient, everlasting?*[139]

Such hope will not assure us. The insurance that God so freely gives secures lifeboats, their rigging and sailors who thwart and redeem us.

---

139. Will last now be first, / although transient, everlasting: see Matt 19:30//Mark 10:31//Luke 13:30.

IF ANIMALS COULD BE CRIMINAL

*A Midrash on Matthew 21:1–11,
Mark 11:1–11, Luke 19:28–44,
and John 12:12–19*

If animals could be criminal we
would consume ourselves, be filled,
then deposit the little we give into
buckets at night, gutters at daylight

when no one is on the street, neither
whores nor those who join with them
nor the draymen who just now yawn
into belief, their wives asleep, their

backs now groaning with the day's
slow crawl into dusk where drinks
await them before heading home.
If animals could be criminal we'd

grab hold of Jesus' triumphal donkey,
throw messiah off, then hurry it to a
house of slaughter as indifferent as
our own. But, if we did this, even we,

even we both humble and serpent
would not dare to wait until its blood
sluiced out into the city's streets.[140]
We would not know whose blood it is.

---

140. Serpent: see Gen 3:1–7, esp. v. 1.

ANTIPODAL SAVAGERIES: JUNE 1, 2020

*A Midrash on Matthew 26:11,
Mark 14:7, and John 12:8*

"For you always have the poor with you."

    —Matthew 26:11[141]

*To The Right Rev. Mariann Budde,
Episcopal Bishop of the Diocese
of Washington, D.C.*[142]

The poor they will always have with
them. But why, Father, will they, two
thousand years hence, exsanguinate my
words so they may ignore your poor

or, even worse, legislate against them?[143]
Why, my Begetter, have you begotten
me,[144] if my words, abused, will only
be sharpened to cut throats, wrists,

and carotids? Those in power, I see,
who will have no care of the gore
coursing through each city's streets,
will also have this only need of me.[145]

---

    141. The quote in its context: "For you always have the poor with you, *but you will not always have me*" (emphasis added).

    142. The Right Rev. Mariann Budde: see nn. 3 and 17.

    143. So they may ignore your poor / or, even worse, legislate against them: see Nathalie Baptiste and Jessica Washington, "Trump Isn't Waging a War on Poverty. He's Waging a War on Poor People," *Mother Jones*, Feb. 14, 2020 (online).

    144. Begotten: see Ps 2:7; Acts 13:33; Heb 1:5; 5:5.

    145. Those in power, I see, / . . . will also have this only need of me: see Evan Osnos, "'An Abuse of Sacred Symbols': Trump, a Bible, and a Sanctuary," *The New Yorker*, June 2, 2020 (online).

FROM SUNUP TO SUN'S REST: DAY 1238 OF THE TRUMP ADMINISTRATION

A Midrash on Numbers 20:1–8

I am here still, from sunup
to sun's rest. Why is Pharaoh
still hammering on the door
when I am always outside in

the wilderness of the LORD's
heart, imploring each rock,
one after another, to open its
womb and give birth to water?

Will Pharaoh ever, because
of his knocking, comprehend
the LORD's sorrows, the pain
that each prevarication causes?

As I wait for this water, I am
guiding the royal vessel on the
sacred Nile.[146] The crowds on the
shore, always obeisant, startle

themselves from subservience
when they understand who now
controls the vessel. Pharaoh
cheers on the praise given him.

---

146. The Nile: see Exodus 1:15–2:4.

THE JUDAS WITHIN

A Midrash on John 20:19–23

Attendant miseries signal both despair
and fellowship as we disciples shelter in
a room. Each whisper of noise is enemy,
Judas returned from the dead to betray us

again. But who, no one dares to ask, is
the Judas *within*? Most of us try to ignore
him. Despite the clawing and scratching
from inside. Within is a sepulcher.[147] Each

of us will have to decide: Do I roll away
the stone[148] or leave it as guardian, not for
Jesus but for the person I thought I had
forgiven, Pilate's and my dearest friend?

---

147. Sepulcher: see Matthew 23:27.
148. Do I roll away / the stone: Matthew 27:55–28:10.

SOFT HEARTS ARE THEIR OWN WHIPS:[149]
A DIALOGUE BETWEEN A MALE
AND A FEMALE DISCIPLE

A Midrash on Psalm 74:18–21[150]

The Trump administration's
successful repeal of Obamacare
"could end health insurance
for some 2.1 million Americans."[151]

Soft hearts are their own whips.
And what of the hard-hearted?
I ask. Will their scourges never
soften? Will they always turn

only on others, striking wounds
birthed from their own? *Wounds*
will heal when those self-stricken
understand. Will each hardened

heart never undress before the
belovèd and, in that undressing,
ask the one, a heart now without
whip, for pardon, then blessing?[152]

---

149. Soft Hearts Are Their Own Whips: a verse from "Excerpts from the Passion," "4. On the Whipping," by David Scott, *Beyond the Drift: New and Selected Poems*, 73. The four poems in "Excerpts from the Passion" are Scott's translations of Latin poems by George Herbert.

150. "Remember this, O Lord, how the enemy scoffs . . . / Do not deliver the soul of your dove to the wild animals; / do not forget the life of your poor forever. / Have regard for your covenant, / for the dark places of the land are full of the haunts of violence. / Do not let the downtrodden be put to shame; let the poor and needy praise your name."

151. Jan Hoffman and Abby Goodnough, "Trump Administration Files Formal Request to Strike Down All of Obamacare," *New York Times*, May 1, 2019 (online).

152. Belovèd: see Matt 3:17//Mark 1:11//Luke 3:22; among many.

Will these our hardened hearts
ever contemplate the touch on
skin that, without mere words,
now forgives? *I hear (I hope)*

*the words you're saying, each
jackal crying at night to a moon
our own. Let us pray that our
predators each lead a battalion*

*that, just before war and war's
embrace, embrace one another.*[153]

---

153. *Predators / . . . embrace one another*: see Isa 11:6–7

SOMETHING AKIN TO VISION

A Midrash on Matthew 16:1–4

"The Pharisees and Sadducees
came and, to test Jesus, asked him
to show them a sign from heaven."

I'm waiting here to see if something
akin to vision will happen my way. By
vision I do not mean what transpires,
and transposes, at night when we are

most alive and least dead. By vision
I mean one syllable, just one, of what
Jesus said earlier this morning in the
marketplace. I heard snatches of words

amid the hubbub and all the taunts
and jeering. But when I drew closer,
so did those dressed fine in undefiled
Temple clothing and, right beside them,

three Roman soldiers, their swords now
drawn. So I backed off, then far away.
What I saw there was both sign and its
wonder, as some of his followers call

them.[154] Jesus removed his outer cloak.
The Temple authorities and soldiers
stopped, with swords still unsheathed.
This Jesus now held up his clothing

---

154. Sign and its / wonder: "signs" and "wonders" are very important in John's Gospel; when Jesus turns water into wine at Cana (John 2:1–11), John calls the miracle "the first of his signs . . . and revealed his glory." Some scholars suggest that John used a "signs source."

to everyone. The authorities backed
off. The Romans remained. He laid
his garment, frayed and mended as it
was, on the offaled and thus unclean

street.[155] The soldiers now withdrew.
The crowd drew closer, expecting
a miracle. When Jesus saw this, he
picked up his cloak. As we gasped

in shock, he tore it in two. Then he
carefully, slowly, sat down and wept.
When he finally raises his head he
sees himself in his mother's womb.

She asks him, Are you ready? *Yes.*

---

155. His garment, frayed and mended: see Joan Taylor, "What Did Jesus Wear?" (Pocket Worthy, online). I wish to thank my colleague Patrick Emmett for this reference.

MAY TONGUES OF FIRE: THE FIRES THIS TIME, PENTECOST SUNDAY, 2020[156]

A Midrash on Genesis 4:1–17

"From life's dawn it is drawn down,
Abel is Cain's brother and breasts
they have sucked the same."

—GERARD MANLEY HOPKINS,
"THE WRECK OF THE DEUTSCHLAND" 20

*To Katy Hanson Harl, former
student, now colleague and friend*

Abel is Cain's suppurating heart,
the wound in each lung, and what
hangs mercenary between his legs.
Why, LORD, we ask, did you not

create woman first? Or, if not then,
why did our Eve not beget woman
anterior, this child at least without
knife or stone, arrowed bow or kiss[157]

siege-fortressing her hand? Cain
with woman trespass-birthed his
son Enoch, then his city.[158] Each
city after burst not into flame but

---

156. "The Fires This Time" borrows from *The Fire Next Time* by James Baldwin (1963) and *The Fire This Time: A New Generation Speaks about Race*, ed. by Jesmyn Ward (2016). See Zeba Blay, "11 James Baldwin Quotes On Race That Resonate Now More Than Ever," *The Huffington Post*, February 3, 2017 (online).

157. Kiss: see Matt 26:47–50//Mark 14:43–50//Luke 22:47–48.

158. Birthed his / son Enoch, then his city: Gen 4:17.

holocaust where dove and lamb
afire cry out to us forever.[159] When
we are able, at last, and fitfully,
some dream of men now-wombed.

When each gives birth, be it girl or
boy, we gather, we sing, not only
in joy, but in forgiveness, for each
child's hands. One hand embraces

the other, then releases. Now each
child cradles another. Holding one
another's hand, together they reach
to suckle Cain's newborn breasts.

May tongues of fire encircle them.[160]

---

159. Holocaust: see nn. 97 and 109.
160. May tongues of fire encircle them: see Acts 2:1–4.

III. LACRIMAE GAUDII[161]

"Very truly, I tell you, you will weep and mourn . . . you will have pain, but your pain will turn into joy."

—John 16:20

---

161. *Lacrimae gaudii*, Latin, means "(the) tears of (or for) joy/happiness/delight."

CHRISTCHILD: A DISCIPLE'S WIDOW CIRCA 60 CE, AFTER A LONG DAY, ENJOYS THE DAY'S WANING LIGHT

A Midrash on Luke 12:3

I sit open-air in spring's evening
sun, outside after a long day within;
the waning light strikes a pot, one I
made only recently. Inside it, a plant

awaits its time to abide, one of the
last. The spider threads know that
they will not be able to capture the
sprout as it, Christchild, rises from

good earth. Because of this, the light
now indwelling each fiber rejoices.
In this rejoicing, rapt, I now behold
these threads, flaming with late light,

doing something not even Moses or
the LORD's prophets could prophesy,
or even imagine: the threads separate.
As they do, a fly begins its resurrection.

THAT FIRST MILK

A Midrash on John 11:16

"Thomas, who was called the Twin,
said to his fellow disciples, 'Let us
also go, that we may die with him.'"

And now the only sorrow that remains
is resurrection. Why are *anástasis* and
thánatos twins?[162] Didymus is my partial
name, thus, "Twin." But my brother lay

dead when I first knew my mother's
breast. When I drank her milk she wept
with joy. She could not know that I saw,
even then, that she also breastfed my

dying lord and savior. As he resurrected
he returned to her blessed. She rejoiced.
She holds me close with one arm; the
other embraces an unbloodied cloth to

wipe the tears from her face. After our
father died, leaving us on our own, she,
as best she could, became my brother and
went with me everywhere, even to distant

Galilee. We wanted to hear this newborn
prophet as he preached God's love. Each
time—yes, each—that Jesus healed, each
time he mothered, exorcising our demons,

---

162. *Anástasis* and *thánatos*: *anástasis* (English "anastasis," though with a very different meaning), from *aná*, "above" or "again," + *stásis*, cognate with *hístēmi*, "to stand," thus "resurrection." *Thánatos*, "death" (English "thanatology"). Both words occur often in the NT.

each time he raised each Lazarus from our
dead,[163] I heard her cry then laugh, rejoice,
as I hadn't growing up within her sorrows
and pain. I see now that she had always

carried him, newborn each day, upon her
back.[164] Are we now near the end? Or is this
our beginning? One day Jesus approached
her and kissed her cheek. He asked her if

he could lift the pack over her arms. Some
now say that he then shouldered her grief
and pain. But I knew even then: No, he
blessed them, turned, then handed them to

me. Then he knelt, took up a handful of dirt,
and spat on it, many times.[165] With this he
anointed us. It was only then that I could
understand: she and I will soon return from

Death's drunken and lustful dance on Skull
Hill.[166] As we walk I will take not only sleeve
but also the hem of my freshworn robe and
wipe dry her face. I will with tears of my own

speak to her of that first milk, long conjoined.

---

163. Each time he raised each Lazarus from our / dead: see John 11:1–44.
164. She had always / carried him, newborn each day, upon her / back: see Matt 16:24//Mark 8:34//Luke 9:23; Matt 11:28–29; Matt 16:24.
165. Then he knelt, took up a handful of dirt, / and spat on it: see John 9:1–12; v. 6.
166. Skull Hill: see Matt 27:23//Mark 15:22//John 19:17. See n. 5.

SILENCE BEARS GOD'S OWN BELIEF

A Midrash on John 20:19–23

The silence that descends and recreates
who we are is never ours in ourselves
but in each other, all others who dwell,
ignorant or not, within God's loves and

fears. Silence. Contemplative silence.[167]
What we know of God, the Creator, our
Sustainer,[168] is, no, not seed. Seed's too
easy: seeds overcome boundaries, and

then dissolve into death and resurrection.
But silence tells us that reawakening is
its own daily death, and the dying before
we breathe our last. Breath,[169] like God,

delivers us, and never alone: after each
pause, each inspiration is resurrection.[170]
Insurrection defines who we are until
our breathing stops. When it starts again

---

167. Contemplative silence: "Contemplative" derives from Latin *contemplatus*, the past participle of *contemplare / contemplari*, "to survey, observe"; *con-* ("with") + *templ(um)*, "space marked off for augural observation, a temple." In my translation efforts, I translate Greek *hēsychía* (English "hesychast," "hesychasm") as "contemplative quiet" or "contemplative silence." A related key word among the early monks is *anápausis* (English "pause"), "inward stillness" (with thanks to Graham Gould for the phrase). See Kenneth Paul Kramer, *Redeeming Time: T. S. Eliot's* Four Quartets.

168. Sustainer: a recent reformulation of "Father, Son, and Holy Spirit" is "Creator, Redeemer, and Sustainer."

169. Breath: Hebrew (*ruach*) and Greek (*pneûma*) mean "wind," "breath," and "spirit." See nn. 102, 187, and 217.

170 Each inspiration is resurrection: there is a play on words here. "Inspiration," now meaning "something inspired," comes by way of Latin *inspirare* "to breathe upon or into." See the previous note. Thus "inspired" is also "in-spirited."

it brings with it a cross—no, not one
blood-riven, but rather one now birthed.
What is birthed dies before it breathes.
Breath in silence bears God's own belief.[171]

---

171. Belief: *pístis*, "faith," is at the heart of *pisteúō*, "to believe" and, importantly, "to believe *in*," "have faith *in*" (Greek *en* and the dative case, or the dative without the preposition), relational and communal, not transactional and actuarial.

EACH EMBRACE NAKED OR CLOTHED: MARCH 10, 2020, THE SECOND WEEK OF LENT

A Midrashic Rebuttal to Deuteronomy 21:22–23.

"When someone is convicted of a crime punishable
by death and is executed, and you hang him on a tree,
his corpse must not remain all night upon the tree; you
shall bury him that same day, for anyone hung on a tree
is under God's curse. You must not defile the land that
the Lord your God is giving you for possession."

Delightful rain, a sudden season
now soddens the earth. In doing
so, it brings forth hope, even when
there is none. But this healing rain

that enlivens even the roadside's
dead weeds tells me that his soon
our resurrection will rejoice with
each undoing we name our own.

The cistern, once dying of thirst,
now calls out to me: *Friend, dear
sister, you may now come drink! My
spirit is yours! This means that yours*

*is now mine—no, not as possession
but as gift, given, and given back.*[172]
They now sit together under a once-
accursed tree and count each leaf's

---

172. In Greek, *cháris* means "favor, grace, gracious care/help, goodwill" and "favor, gracious deed/gift, benefaction," and the cognate *chárisma* means "gift" (Bauer 1079a-b).

abounding generosity. Benedictions will tonight bring the new moon and, tomorrow, the sun, our shield.[173] Each embrace, naked or clothed, now ours.

---

173. The sun, our shield: "For the LORD God is a sun and shield" (Ps 84:11).

AGAINST THE MEAN

A Midrash on Psalm 50:11

"I know all the birds of the air,
and all that moves in the field is mine."

The sorrows, or delights, that one
bird singing brings to another seem
beyond our ken, yet we, somehow,
against the mean, know its meaning.

THE LIZARD AND ITS BONES

A Midrash on Exodus 14:1–21

The best imprisonment, one that gives
life, is never jailers' but always ours,
alone, when by ourselves we dare bear
silence to our tongues. Speech is now

each wall, humid, scarified, not talking
to others, only to itself, proud of its
shackles and leg irons, its bloodstains.
Jesus now arrives near the end of our

beginning. We shout *Hosannas!* that
strike the walls, break off fragments
that have witnessed men go off to bone.
Jesus looks to the pieces, then to us.

We expect a parable, a story, perhaps
one that speaks of walls and their soon
undoing, the blood remaining in arm and
leg irons. But no, instead of kneeling

to draw on the ground, as we saw him
do many times,[174] he goes to a corner.
Despite our protests he seats himself
beside the bucket. In obedience, it

overflows. To our astonishment, he
plunges his hand in this offal and its
every kind of uncleanness. He is silent.
He somehow parts our carrion debris.[175]

---

174. Kneeling / to draw on the ground: see John 7:53–8:11.
175. Parts: see Exod 14:21–22.

From beneath his dim shadow emerges
in the partings somehow a lizard. But—
it's bereft of its bones. We all startle at
its yet-insistent, feeble movement. As it

crawls through tide pools, rocks, and
shallows, it stops to gather bones at
each eruption, each excrescence. Now
whole, it offers thanks for deliverance.

THE GATE WITHIN CHRIST'S AGORA

A Midrash on Matthew 6:26–29
and Luke 12:24–28

It's usually at the end, when
the lilies of the field and the
birds that enflesh our air for
us draw near, then nearer.

Only then, prayer shawls on,
our phylacteries warding off
present and future sin, only
then, which is the Presence,[176]

only then dare we begin to
assemble at the gate within
Christ's agora. Lepers, and
those without limbs, kept by

the priests distant, now draw
near, nearer than the jugular
vein in our necks.[177] It's now,
at this terminus, its inception,

---

176. Presence: *Shekhinah* (Hebrew *šekīnah*), spelled various ways, denotes the dwelling or settling of the divine presence of God. The term, from rabbinic literature, does not occur in the Bible. The Semitic root is *sh-kh-n*, "to settle, inhabit, or dwell." The verb often refers to the dwelling of a person or animal, or to the dwelling of God. Nouns derived from the root include *shachen*, "neighbor," and *mishkan*, a dwelling-place, a home or a holy site such as the Tabernacle. In classic Jewish thought, the shekhinah refers to a dwelling or settling in a special sense, of divine presence. A feminine word, shekhinah represents the feminine attributes of the presence of God, especially in the Talmud (Wikipedia, adapted), similar to "Lady" Wisdom in Prov 8.

177. Nearer than the jugular / vein in our necks: Qur'ān 50:16.

that we begin and, thus, end.
Only then, only now, will we
kiss the leper's sore, embrace
the limbtorn skin. Only then,

now, will we welcome one,
then another, into our home,
up to our table. Now clothed
against our darkness, its blight,

we can join hands. Each hand
informs us of our bodies' sweat.
This speaks of its closeness, our
before-now unseen tenderness.

THE CURE OF SOULS:
WRITTEN IN A TIME OF PLAGUE[178]

A Midrash on Matthew 28:1–10,
Mark 16:1–8, and Luke 24:1–8

To the other clergy of
Grace-St. Paul's, 2007–2017:
Anne, Cindy, Deb, Vern

I. Sublunary Ministrations

An angel beaten is still an angel,
now defeated and triumphant, and,
as angel, soon memorialized, then
forgotten. Dare we define these felt

monuments by open incisions and
what angels now must remember?
What forgettings does our God hope
for our messengers?[179] As angels first

volunteer for sublunary ministrations
each knows that most returning return
first severed then restored, Death's
head carried cross-girt on each back.

---

178. The cure of souls: an archaic translation of Latin *cura animarum*, "care of souls" describes the ministry of clergy. Steven Croft, Anglican Bishop of Oxford: "The cure of souls . . . is . . . of the whole parish . . . The term cure means more than care (although all cure of souls is built on love). At its centre is the ministry of reconciliation between individuals and God and between people and communities . . ." (Diocese of Oxford, Bishop Steven's blog).

179. Messengers: *ángellos*, "angel," means "messenger."

II. The Recovery of First Flight

Each angel first watches the entrance
to a tomb. When another comes, this
first must then descend into one of our
discarded museums. Dare we within

throw open the doors? Dare we here
welcome our newborn visitor? Now
another angel waits outside, then one
more. Each stands mendicant, praises

the birth of each risen soul now outside,
then flies to its new God-given ministry.
There, angels' feathers distanced from
follicle arise, recovering our first flight.

DANCE THAT YOU MAY BECOME

A Midrash on Psalm 150:1–6

When angels' wings become
too heavy because of us, the
demons draw near, feasting;
nits and parasites simulacra

our sins. They now ask *Who
begets us?*[180] Each angel now
burnt-feathered, once balmed
offers reply, *Begetting is the*

*Lord's. We, begotten, dare
fly.*[181] *When flame comes, we
sing. Our song is now yours.
Dance, that you may become.*

---

180. They [the demons] ask *Who / begets us?*: another reading could be "They [nits and parasites] ask *Who / begets us?*"
181. Begotten: see Ps 2:7 (NRSV); John 1:14, 18; 3:16, 18 (KJV).

EACH TREE EACH VINE

A Midrash on Romans 5:1–4

March 26, 2020
COVID-19 Deaths in
the U.S. Approach 1,000

I am so distant from the hope
of myself.[182] Yes, of course, I
hold hope in my outstretched
hands, as I now hold dear our

starvelings, all those despised.
Or a child newborn, And, yet,
I remain so distant from the
hope that I would, believe me,

have indwell, vines I would
plant and tenderly viniculture,
olive trees generations old
whose trunks split in two, or

even three, and yet they remain
whole—I see now: even more
whole. Or is it even more than
whole? Each tree, each vine, is

hope, I now see. Isn't this so?
Despair, I begin to understand,
carries an axe, then a bloodened
saw. I disarm him. He kisses me.

---

182. Mary Oliver, "When I Am Among the Trees," *Devotions: The Selected Poems of Mary Oliver*, 123.

EACH BONE WILL FIND ITS LOST BODY: A DISCIPLE QUERIES JESUS

A Midrash on Psalm 104:16

A wilderness of darkness draws me to
you. The cedars of Lebanon, transfigured
to desert, glow like fireflies within fallen
night.[183] I watch Satan go from one to still

another, trying to warm his hands. Yet
they remain frostbitten, frozen so tight
that, when each dies, carrion birds peck
repeatedly at it for their food, yet they

fail. Failure comes more quickly when
there is no light. Death finds night more
rewarding: demons dance more assuredly,
wearing bone necklaces that toss, leap,

and wing, each bone a soul begging you
for its release. You're waiting here for
sunrise, you say. But what good is that?
Listen. Do you hear hawks singing each

to each?[184] *It's not what you think. They
dance and celebrate now that their prey
give us birth. Don't you hear it? Each
bird has a bone in its mouth. Just before*

---

183. The cedars of Lebanon: see 1 Kgs 5:6; Ps 29:5; Isa 2:13.
184. Do you hear hawks singing each / to each: see T. S. Eliot, "The Love Song of J. Alfred Prufrock": "I have heard the mermaids singing, each to each. / I do not think they will sing to me."

sunrise, each bone will find its lost body.
Bone to bone will then beget soul. Soul
will then sing. As song concludes, Satan
will present his hands, shriven, and whole.

THE ACTS OF PAUL

I. One Loaf One Fish: Paul
Imprisoned in Philippi of Macedonia

A Midrash on Acts 16:16–24

Only one flower bloomed here
this bud-time. So I began my
despair. Then I realized that,
cut, I can bring it to the two

conscripts standing guard
outside my gate. So I'm now
planting it in the dust between
their feet: one loaf, one fish.[185]

II. The Last Days of Paul:
Two Recollections, c. 60 CE

1.
Now She Sits Beside Me:
After Writing Two Letters,
Now Lost, Paul Reflects

*A Midrash on 1 Thessalonians 1:6
and Galatians 3:1–18*

Do you see the parchment copy
of my fears lying on the table?
Do you see what lies beside it?
A sheet of papyrus, my faith and

---

185. One loaf, one fish: see Matt 14:13–21//Mark 6:31–44//Luke 9:12–17//John 6:1–14.

belief. My amanuensis, reluctant
from the start, having written, has
fled.[186] I, for one, don't blame him.
Now in Rome, captive, I will soon

be dead. How do I know this? you
ask. I have often written to you,
and others, and to myself, about
the Holy Spirit.[187] Although we were

belovèd, I often felt her distance.
Now she sits beside me, her left
hand holding mine, her right arm
tenderly across my now-flayed

shoulders. Now she kisses my
torn cheek. Discomfited, I hold
the other away from her lest she
feel in my imprisonment fear.[188]

2.
I Would in My Love: A Christian
In Rome Around the Year 60
Reflects on Paul's Death

A Midrash on Romans 12:19

A cascading fire brimmed, then
consumed me. Not only me but
our whole tribe, the few of us
not already lost to contagion,

---

186. My amanuensis: see Rom 16:22.
187. Holy Spirit: see Rom 5:5; 1 Cor 6:19; 1 Thess 1:5; among many. On spirit/the Spirit as *ruach* see nn. 102, 169, and 217.
188. My imprisonment: see Acts 28:16.

its slaughter. Massacre has to
begin somewhere, and with
someone. When someone lies
now without blood, there are

no mourners: they've all fled.
He said, *Let the dead now bury
their dead.*[189] We implored him
to tell us what he meant. Our

question and his answer were
not recorded, so both are now
dying with us where the dead
bury their resurrected, then ask

for their forgiveness. *Vengeance
is mine, says the Lord.*[190] Our Paul
wrote this to us but, we're told,
before he died for our sins,[191] he

regretted his words, or at least the
ones misused by us.[192] Tomorrow,
we bury him, at night, despite
the pestilence that darkness brings,

its remembrances and our failed
attempts at understanding. With Paul
now dead, God tells us, for the first
time, *If I were to remember every*

---

189. Let the dead now bury / their dead: Matt 8:22//Luke 9:60.

190. Vengeance / is mine, says the Lord: Rom 12:19 (KJV). NRSV: "Beloved, never avenge yourselves, but leave room for the wrath of God; for it is written, 'Vengeance is mine, I will repay, says the Lord.'"

191. Before he died for our sins: 1 Pet 3:18.

192. words . . . / misused by us: see "Antipodal Savageries," p. 81.

failure where you live and move and
have your being,[193] *I would, in my love*
for you, never again open my eyes.
Now blind, I would see much further.

III. Streams of Our Beginning: A Dialogue Between Christ and Paul of Tarsus

A Midrash on Galatians 1:11–16 and Acts 9:9–19

I feel such great joy. Dismemberment has been my sight and hearing for so long now that the sleeves of my tunic shred when I touch them, the thorn

taken from my side, though withdrawn, still bleeds and entreats you to stop its bleeding.[194] I stand now for prayer. *Do you see that prayer is both mine and*

yours? But what, then, is yours, alone, so far, yet always so near? Are you both this thorn and its flow of blood?[195] Why now this silence, Lord? My deafness

will continue in its failure if you do not answer. *What do you hear now, Paul, found friend? What do you see with eyes long so damaged? Tell me, so I may*

---

193. Where you live and move and / have your being: Acts 17:28.
194. The thorn: see 2 Cor 12:6–12.
195. Flow of blood: see Matt 9:20–22//Mark 5:25–34//Luke 8:43–48.

offer rest.[196] *It has been so long since I
have been able to rest. Sorrowed by all
I see, even the Sabbath, Shabbat shalom,*[197]
will not open its doors for me. A home

*is what I seek. When I felt your new-
found joy—you see, I do believe you—
and saw you rise in prayer, I had my
doubts. Michael and Gabriel stood to*

*reassure me. On each side they touched
my shoulders. When I, at last, discerned
their touch, I understood. My joy, after
such prolonged grieving, is now yours.*

*Yours, though incipient, lies in the warp
and woof of your tunic, now whole. The
thorn—you will need to trust me here—
will, yes (I am now holding your face),*

*always be yours, and will always bleed.
But this bleeding will also bring with it
rivers that rejoice, lambs now made whole
that gambol in streams of our beginning.*

---

196. Rest: see n. 167.
197. Shabbat shalom: "a Sabbath of peace," a greeting Jews give one another on the Sabbath.

THIS NEW SABBATH:
AFTER SCOTT CAIRNS, "THE DEATH OF MOSES"[198]

A Midrash on Exodus 4:1–31

April 4, 2020: the Feast Day
of Martin Luther King, Jr.[199]

I need to leave now and place
all barbarisms on my tongue,
be they Egyptian or Canaanite,
abrasives that tear my palate

to shreds. Only by doing this
will I escape your unexplained
wrath.[200] I will be very sure to tell
Aaron nothing.[201] Midian will be

my only tongue now, one that
you, LORD, no longer understand.
You speak only Hebrew now,
a language I will comprehend

on Mt. Pisgah[202] when you,
once again, pour out molten
lead at me in anger that, here,
at the end, I will refuse to bear.

---

198. Cairns, *Slow Pilgrim: The Collected Poems*, 145.

199. King's feast day in the Episcopal Church is April 4, the day of his martyrdom.

200. Wrath: religious stories about God or the sacred use anthropomorphic language. God, like us, loves, and God hates, and also has uncontrollable anger, showing the inherent limitation of language in expressing the inexpressible. See Exod 4:14; Isa 5:25; Heb 4:3; Rev 14:10; among many.

201. I will be very sure to tell / Aaron nothing: see Exod 32:1–6.

202. Mt. Pisgah: see Deut 3:23–39.

I will die here on Pisgah. But
my bones, despite what is said,
will not lie in Moab, opposite
Beth-peor. No, after our Joshua

and his people move on far into
Canaan, the bones on Pisgah
will arise. They will walk, one
by living one, until they reach

the bones, all still inherent with
flesh, of all those whom Joshua
has killed. We will gather them
and sew onto them deliverance.

Free at last, now born, we will no
longer strip flesh from bone.[203] We
will promise to the LORD, and to
one another, that we, now undone,

will no longer excavate slaughter
from stone, each rubble a wound.
We will knead anger into bread
that no longer bleeds when torn.

---

203. In the closing words of his speech at the March on Washington on August 28, 1963, Martin Luther King intoned "Free at last. Free at last. Thank God Almighty, we are free at last" (text and video online).

ONLY ABSOLVED DARE WE CONFESS

A Midrash on Matthew 6:23 and Luke 11:36

To Greg Boyle, S.J.,
Barking to the Choir[204]

The Lord warns us to take care that
the light within not be darkness—or,
at least, not the only darkness, and its
light. What we confess. Confession

in the Lord's sight always follows
absolution. Only absolved dare we
confess. If this were not so, the man
born not blind but long blinded by

us[205] would have failed to see at birth
from his mother's womb the womb's
darkness, that light that God made in
the beginning.[206] That beginning, now

a brilliance, first sought out our God
in order to ask: *May I shine, always,*
without dark's blindness? The Lord
holds out one hand, then the other.

---

204. *Barking to the Choir: The Power of Radical Kinship* (2018). Greg Boyle and two men from Homeboy Industries gave the annual Kegley lecture at CSU Bakersfield on November 13, 2018; the video is available on YouTube.

205. The man / once born not blind but blinded by / us: see John 9:1–41.

206. That light that God made in / the beginning: see Gen 1:3–4; John 1:1–5.

HIS WILDERNESS WITHIN

A Midrash on Matthew 4:1–11
Mark 1:12, and Luke 4:1–12

To Paul Quenon, OCSO
Amounting to Nothing: Poems

I'm gasping for air. No, I'm not
drowning—yet. I'm lying in what
passes here for a bed, ticking that
always speaks to me of manure.

The smell from the courtyard
where we gather the animals at
night, safe from what always
troubles them, now troubles me.[207]

Jesus has left us here to go—
where? Our writings will later
say that he went off by himself,
into some filial and undefined

wilderness.[208] So why won't they
talk to us? No one will ask me,
but I think that his wilderness
is, in fact, within, in each of us.

---

207. Courtyard: *aulé*, used also as a sheepfold at night. The cognate verb *aulízomai* means to stay someplace temporarily.

208. Wilderness: *érēmos* means both "wilderness" and "desert," the wilderness of Moses, John the Baptist, Jesus and, later, early Christian monastics. In the NRSV, John 1:14 states, "And the Word became flesh and lived among us" (KJV: "dwelt"). "Lived" and "dwelt" translate *skēnóō*, "to pitch a tent" (*skēné*, English "scene," from Greek drama).

What always frightens us—yes,
it terrifies me—is that in this
waste expanse, despite all that
we pray and all that we ask, there

is no courtyard, no gate, no—if
we dare admit it—no house where
we can sequester and find shelter.
But flames at sunset now break

through the gaps and windows in
walls that aren't here.[209] Jesus returns.
He carries a burning bush in each
hand: they enkindle our wilderness.[210]

---

209. The gaps and windows in / walls that aren't here: see John 19:19–20.
210. Burning bush: Exod 3:1–5.

BIRTHED FROM GOD'S WOMB

A Midrash on John 14:15–17, 26; 15:26

The Paraclete now begins her dance.[211]
Since she is our Comforter, she calls
to her partner, the Advocate. She, too,
joins the dance. Angels and archangels

clap their hands.[212] Even Satan, at last
hallowing God's victory, begins to
sing! His song, though, is rusty, as if
a scythe or Roman sword had lain too

long in sun and rain and decomposed
now into jeers. All our dancers here,
clapping their hands and singing, are
fully aware of this. They each now vie

to take his hand, to make him their
partner. Now the Paraclete, belovèd
and lover, joins the throng.[213] Satan,
stunned, begins his fall to the ground.

---

211. Paraclete . . . / Comforter: *paráklētos*, occuring only in John's Gospel, combines the preposition *pará*, "beside" (as in "paralegal") and the verb *kaléō*, "to call." *Parakaléō* means "to ask to come and be present where the speaker is, call to one's side," "urge, exhort, encourage," "comfort, encourage, cheer up." In Greek law, a *paráklētos* was one's advocate in court, the person who stood by your side in support. Thus, for *paráklētos* translations use "Comforter," "Intercessor, Helper," or "Advocate."

212. Angels and archangels: see 1 Thess 4:16.

213. Belovèd / and lover: "Belovèd" is *agapētós*, in the NT, cognate with *agápē*, "love," and *agapáō*, "to love." The three together occur well over 200 times.

Held and saved by the now-bleeding women, he accepts each flow of blood as his own. He now experiences each childbirth of those whom he afflicted.

His birthed from God's torn womb.[214]

---

214. God's womb: Hebrew "compassion" is etymologically related to "womb."

EACH BODY WHOLE: A DIALOGUE

A Midrash on John 1:1–5 and John 12:36

The jackdaws here commiserate:
their sufferings his—and ours.

Impossibility? Let's now consider
this: God's own son, from Galilee.

And... Yes, Galilee is our back
of beyond, even further than that.

Do you mock me, friend? Or are
you enemy, Roman, deep in wine?

Enemies and friends. Isn't each
a death-black wing on these birds?

I hear, at best, lost riddles in your
words; at worst, a lofty contempt.

No, friend, you've misunderstood.
One wing is Satan, the other Christ.

And the body in between, never in
flight, always pulled into shreds?

Ah, yes. Thank you. The jackdaw's
body, ours, often is. Do you see?

Yes... I think. But... No. I don't
want to! Unless—can sight whiten?

Some. Sight is friend to wilderness.[215]
Necessary. And also partial, always.

Yet insight and compassion can ferry
us, together, over treacherous shoals.

Once on land, almost wracked, then
ruined, we see that light is darkness,

and darkness its own light. Here Spirit
sits naked, next to a soon-emptied tomb.[216]

She waits for escort.[217] When the angels at
last alight, the right wing of one is white,

the left one black. The left wing of one is
white, the other black. Each body whole.

---

215. Wilderness: Greek *erēmos* means both "wilderness" and "desert," the wilderness of Moses, John the Baptist, Jesus and, later, early Christian monastics.

216. A soon-emptied tomb: see Mark 16:1–8//Matt 28:1–10//Luke 24:1–8//John 20:1–13.

217. She: in Hebrew, *ruach*, "wind," "breath," "spirit," is a feminine noun. See nn. 102, 169, and 187.

A SINGLE PIECE OF SKIN

*A Midrash on Matthew 14:13–21,
Mark 6:31–44, Luke 9:12–17, and John 6:1–14*

What can I do for all of these
people? I now admit, to myself,
then to you, that my very first
thought—or was it feeling?—

was What can I *do* with all of
these people? The lepers among
them cover everything but their
eyes. Many think these anathema[218]

blind. Both they and I know—
which means you do, too—that
this blindness is only the failed
eyesight of all those around them

who clamor that they've come to
be part of your Kingdom. They
imagine and, possibly, believe
that in order to make their way

to you (they are taught), they
must bring pitchforks and axes,
hammers and adzes, in order
to find their way in. These our

---

218. Anathema: Greek *anáthema* originally meant "a votive offering, thing dedicated, set apart," in a sacred sense, to or for a god or gods, but then came to mean "separated, accursed." So then "of people officially pronounced accursed or separated from the Church either in life or after death" (Lampe 102b). Latin *profanum* (English "profane"), originally meant "before/in front of, thus outside, away from" (*pro-*), a temple (*fanum*). See 1 Cor 12:3; 16:22; Gal 1:8–9; Rom 9:3. The first version of the Nicene Creed (325 CE) ended with five anathemas against those whom the Council deemed heretics. See "The Nicene Creed," Wikipedia.

lepers have made their way to us
with only a single piece of skin.
They hand it to the gatekeeper
who will never be there. He now

cleanses it, hands it back to each,
opens the gate, welcoming them.

AS THE HOLY DOVE NOW DESCENDS

*A Midrash on Numbers 20:1–11, Matthew 3:13–17,
Mark 1:9–11, and Luke 3:21–22*

I once sought out the transparencies
of sin, but no longer. I now eat from
donkeys' troughs and the dust that
resurrects when the rich throw bones

to the dogs in their courtyards. The
screams of carrion birds in Death's sky
will not surrender. Our corpses hang
still on crosses, even after we take

each down and give him honorable
burial and each interment's prayers.
I no longer weep at the sight of each
cross. I'm sorry—I can't. The last

time I wept, my tears, scalding, burned
me as though I were in Sinai's desert
begging for drops of water.[219] But . . .
my tears now enflesh: each tells me

Moses struck rock and brought forth
deliverance; the Baptist rejoiced *and*
wept when baptizing Jesus. As the
Holy Dove now descends, I welcome

her and comfort her in my hands. Her
each tear now Jordan's healing waters.

---

219. My tears, scalding, burned /me as though I were in Sinai's desert / begging for drops of water: see Luke 16:19–31.

DEEP GLOWERING CLOUDS NOW LEAVING

A Midrash on Genesis 6–9

A very black spider—no, not
the onyx of night but rather
the obsidian void of Hades—
this spider, without guilt, of

course, attacked me without
my knowledge. But I, who am
learnèd, a scribe of the Gospel
of, and for, Lord Jesus Christ,

have now to ask: After what
word on this still-drying page
did its bite, perhaps just now,
kill me? I had just then started

to transcribe John's immaculate
Gospel. *In the beginning*[220] speaks
to me of a time long before the
misspent garden,[221] long before the

flood that I, now bit, fully know
that God, weeping and wailing,
came to repent. Yes, I now feel
fever. Fearful, I drop my pen. In

that letting go, before the pen hits
the Lord's own table, something
sounds: I see God somehow unflood
the earth. Each animal that our sins

---

220. In the beginning: John 1:1 (Gen 1:1).
221. The / misspent garden: see Gen 2:4b–3:24.

(yes) killed,²²² every living creature
that moves, every kind, with which
the waters swarm, and every wingèd
bird of every kind—I now watch

each of them swim, crawl, and leap
from God's new-resplendent waters.²²³
Each, now endowed with Pentecost
tongue,²²⁴ reveals to our God that the

grasses of the fields, the trees with
their leaves, the flowers that give us
birth, must also come forth, or they
die and return to water once dead.

God now sits. The LORD begins to
weep. The LORD knows that what the
angels are saying is true. In his long-
distilling anger, acrimony unrequited,

he had never questioned the undoing.
This realization, he now understands,
is the light that has always informed
deep glowering clouds now leaving.

    222. Each animal that our sins / (yes) killed: see Gen 6:5–7.
    223. Every living creature that / moves . . . / every wingèd / bird of every kind: Gen 1:20–21.
    224. Each, now endowed with Pentecost / tongue: see Acts 2:1–11.

THE LORD'S ALWAYS EMPTY THRONE

*A Midrash on Matthew 8:23–27,
Mark 4:35–41, Luke 8:22–25*

We have about an hour until the storm
subsides. Jesus, at the front of the boat,
says nothing. So be it. Maybe Gennesaret
will also add us to its storehouse of bones

stripped by fish, those who feed us. We,
with neither sword nor shield nor spear,
nevertheless hunt beneath this lake. I cry
out: Does a storm, like a pillar of salt,[225]

or a bush's sacred flames,[226] tell us more
than the waves and maledictions here that,
mocking us, cavort and play upon this, the
LORD's waters? Do the seabirds, absent,

on shore, jeer? Will the LORD, who bosoms
bird, wave, and bone, hear our cries and
draw near? *Nearness is the LORD's always
empty throne.* But how can we, through all

this tempest, admire the gold-inlaid wings
of cherubim and seraphim,[227] their dancing?
*Listen! Hearing our cries that, to them, are
hoarse cries in battle, they now suddenly*

---

225. A pillar of salt: see Gen 19:24–26.
226. A bush's sacred flames: see Exod 3:1–6.
227. Cherubim and seraphim: see Exod 25:17–22; Isa 6:1–8; Ezek 10:1–22.

stop. Despite the rain, they descend, each
wing now flame. And now, hosts of angels
come down to save us, fled from war and
rumor of war.[228] Each is blind. The LORD

heals them as the storms devouring us end.
And now—the seas are calm! Jesus looks to
us. He nods. We begin to haul in each half-
drowned messenger.[229] Each begins to sing.[230]

---

228. War and / rumor of war: Matt 24:6//Mark 13:7. One of the best books on the Vietnam War is *A Rumor of War* by Philip Caputo.

229. Messenger: the original meaning of *ángellos* is "messenger."

230. Each begins to sing: see Exod 15:20–21; Pss 5:11; 26:7; among many.

Scripture Index

OLD TESTAMENT/ HEBREW BIBLE

Genesis

1:1	128
1:2	47
1:3–4	118
1:20–21	129
2:4b–3:24	128
2:20	25
3:1–7	80
3:17–19	12
3:21	68
3:24	69
4:1–17	88
4:17	41, 88
6–9	128
6:5–7	129
8:8–12	38
9:8–17	68
18:6–19:29	66
19:24–26	130
28:10–22	52

Exodus

1:15–2:4	82
3:1–6	130
3:1–5	120
3:13–15	xx
4:1–31	116
4:14	116
14:1–21	101
14:11	67
14:21–22	101
14:26–31	73
15:1	73
15:20–21	131
17:1–7	66
20:21	56
20:24	64
25:17–22	130
28:1–4	36
28:41	36
29:14	64
32	36
32:1–6	116

Leviticus

1:1–17	64
1:10–11	56
18:21	62
20:2–5	62

Numbers

20:1–11	127
20:1–8	82

Deuteronomy

3:23–39	116
6:4	8
21:22–23	98
21:23	58
28:20	45
28:24	74
28:28–29	45
28:38–43	73

SCRIPTURE INDEX

Joshua
6	56, 64
8	64
8:1–31a	13
10:1–15	63

2 Samuel
11:1–27	58

1 Kings
5:6	109
10:1–13	73

2 Kings
2:1–12	74
22:14–20	62

2 Chronicles
34:22–28	62

Job
33:28	78

Psalms
2:7	81, 107
5:11	131
8	11
26:7	131
29:5	109
50:11	100
55:6	39
68:13	39
74:18–21	43, 84
74:19	39
84:11	99
104:16	109
150:1–6	107

Proverbs
8	103

Isaiah
2:13	109
5:25	116
6:1–8	130
11:6–7	85

Jeremiah
1:5	29
2:23	62
7:9	62
8:1–2	62
9:22	62
16:4	62
19:15	62
25:33	62
38:1–6	62

Lamentations
1–5	16
1:2	17
1:12	17

Ezekiel
10:1–22	130
37:1–14	4

Joel
1:1–12	73

Malachi
4:5–6	74

NEW TESTAMENT

Matt
2:9–14	22
3:13–17	127
3:16	38
3:17	84
4:1–11	119
4:25	9
5:1	9
5:22	31
5:29–30	31
6:19–21	35

6:23	118	28:1	16
6:26–29	103	28:1–10	33, 35, 37, 105, 124
6:28–29	40	28:2	6
7:13	31		
7:28	9	**Mark**	
8:1–4	71	1:9–11	127
8:14–15	71	1:10	38
8:22	113	1:11	84
8:23–27	130	1:12	119
9:20–26	71	1:29–31	71
9:20–22	114	3:1–6	22
9:36	60	4:35–41	130
10:28	31	5:21–43	71
11:7–9	9	5:25–34	114
11:28–29	95	6:31–44	111, 125
13:38–42	31	6:34	60
14:13–21	111, 125	8:34	95
16:1–4	86	9:2–8	47
16:24	95	9:18	21
16:25	48	9:42	7
17:1–20	47	10:25	35
18:6–7	7	10:27	9
19:24	35	10:31	41, 79
19:26	9	11:1–11	80
19:30	41, 79	12:41–44	50
21:1–11	80	13:1–2	46, 76
22:1–14	41	13:7	131
22:39	58	14:7	81
23:27	83	14:12–26	20
24:1–2	46	14:21–41	70
24:6	131	14:43–50	12, 88
25:31–40	22	14:44–45	5
26:11	81	14:50	12, 13, 37
26:17–30	20	15:21	4
26:47–56	12	15:22	4, 95
26:47–50	88	15:36	20
26:48–49	5	15:40	4, 16, 20, 32, 35, 37
26:56	12, 13, 19	16:1–8	37, 105, 124
27:3–6	6	16:1	16, 20, 37
27:23	95	16:8	21
27:32–56	70	16:9	35
27:32	4	26:3–5	6
27:33	4		
27:48	20	**Luke**	
27:50	3	1:76	9
27:55–28:10	83	2:7	57
27:55–56	4, 20, 32, 35		
27:56	16		

Luke (continued)

3:21–22	38, 127
3:22	84
3:38	13
4:1–12	119
4:38–41	71
7:1–10	71
8:2–3	35
8:22–25	130
8:40–56	37, 71
8:43–48	114
9:12–17	111, 125
9:23	95
9:28–36	47
9:60	113
10:25–37	58
11:36	118
12:3	93
12:24–28	103
12:27	40
13:30	79
13:34	76
14:1–6	22
14:7–12	41
16:19–31	40, 52, 65, 127
16:20–21	41
17:1–2	7
18:25	35
18:27	9
19:28–44	80
21:5–6	46
22:7–39	20
22:47–62	12
22:47–48	5, 88
23:26–49	70
23:26	4
23:36	20
23:46	3
23:49	4, 20, 32
23:54–56	35
23:56	20
24:1–12	34, 37
24:1–10	35
24:1–8	105, 124
24:1	20
24:2–4	6
24:10	16
24:13–35	39
24:13–14	39
24:39–40	18
24:44–49	60

John

1:1–9	29
1:1–5	118, 123
1:1	128
1:5	21
1:14	107, 119
1:18	107
1:32	38
2:1–11	8, 86
3:16	107
3:18	107
4:1–7	15
4:43–54	71
6:1–14	111, 125
7:53–8:11	101
8:1–11	41, 75
8:3	21
9:1–41	118
9:1–12	95
9:40	20
11:1–44	95
11:16	94
12:8	81
12:12–19	80
12:36	123
13:1–17:26	20
14:15–17	121
14:26	121
15:26	121
16:20	91
18:1–11	12
18:15–18	12
19:17–37	70
19:17	4, 95
19:19–20	120
19:25	4, 16, 20, 32, 35
19:29	20
19:30	3
19:32–34	70
19:34	14
20:1–13	124
20:1	16, 35

20:17	28
20:19–23	83, 96
20:19	37

Acts

1:16–20	6
2:1–11	129
2:1–4	34, 89
9:9–19	114
13:33	81
16:16–24	111
16:26	8
17:28	114
21:33	8
25:25	21
26:29	8
28:16	112

Romans

2:7	5
5:1–4	108
5:5	112
5:12–14	12, 13
6:23	5
9:3	125
9:30	21
12:19	112, 113
16:22	112

1 Corinthians

6:19	112
9:24	21
12:3	125
15:3	33, 41
15:22	13
15:26	24
16:22	125

2 Corinthians

12:6–12	114

Galatians

1:8–9	125
1:11–16	114
3:1–18	111
3:6–9	xii, 7

Ephesians

4:9	26
6:5–6	50
6:12	28

Philippians

3:5	7

Colossians

1:16	28
3:22	50

1 Thessalonians

1:5	112
1:6	111
4:16	121

1 Timothy

2:13–14	13

Hebrews

1:5	81
4:3	116
5:5	81

1 Peter

3:18	113
4:6	26

Revelation

14:10	116

www.ingramcontent.com/pod-product-compliance
Lightning Source LLC
Chambersburg PA
CBHW051110160426
43193CB00010B/1385